THE EASY FOLKSONG FAKE BOOK

Melody, Lyrics and Simplified Ch

C000121697

Over 120 Songs | **THE** | **In the Key of "C"**

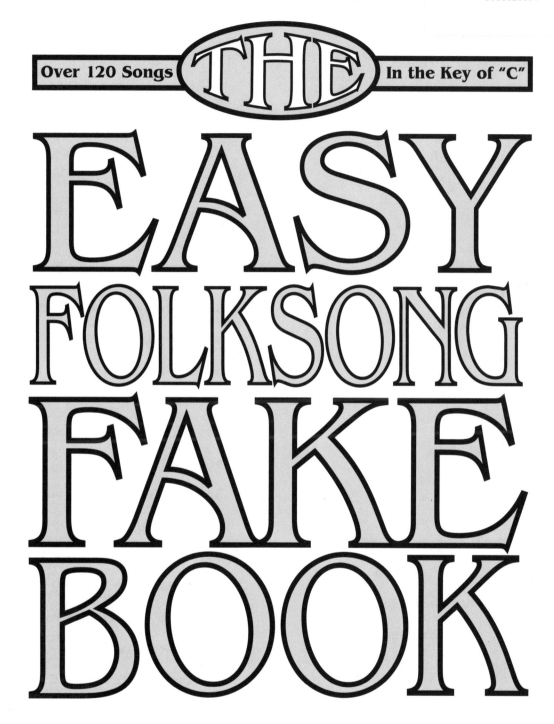

EASY FOLKSONG FAKE BOOK

ISBN 978-1-4234-9903-9

HAL•LEONARD®
CORPORATION
7777 W. BLUEMOUND RD. P.O. BOX 13819 MILWAUKEE, WI 53213

In Australia Contact:
Hal Leonard Australia Pty. Ltd.
4 Lentara Court
Cheltenham, Victoria, 3192 Australia
Email: ausadmin@halleonard.com.au

Visit Hal Leonard Online at
www.halleonard.com

THE EASY FOLKSONG FAKE BOOK

CONTENTS

INTRODUCTION

What Is a Fake Book?

A fake book has one-line music notation consisting of melody, lyrics and chord symbols. This lead sheet format is a "musical shorthand" which is an invaluable resource for all musicians—hobbyists to professionals.

Here's how *The Easy Folksong Fake Book* differs from most standard fake books:

- All songs are in the key of C.

- Only five basic chord types are used—major, minor, seventh, diminished and augmented.

- The music notation is larger for ease of reading.

In the event that you haven't used chord symbols to create accompaniment, or your experience is limited, a chord speller chart is included at the back of the book to help you get started.

Have fun!

A-TISKET A-TASKET

Traditional

Moderately

A - tis - ket, a - tas - ket, a green and yel - low bas - ket, I

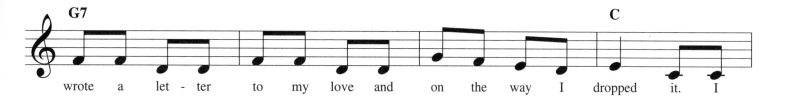

wrote a let - ter to my love and on the way I dropped it. I

dropped it, I dropped it, and on the way I dropped it. A

lit - tle {boy / girl} picked it up and put it in {his / her} pock - et.

ALL GOD'S CHILDREN GOT SHOES

African-American Spiritual

ALL NIGHT, ALL DAY

African-American Spiritual

Day is dy - in' in _____ the west, an - gels watch - in' o - ver
Now I lay me down ___ to sleep, an - gels watch - in' o - ver
love stay with me through _ the night, an - gels watch - in' o - ver

me, my Lord. __ Sleep, my child, and take __ your rest,
me, my Lord. __ Pray the Lord my soul __ to keep,
me, my Lord. __ And wake me with the morn - ing light,

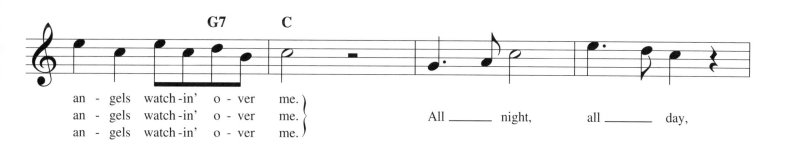

an - gels watch -in' o - ver me.
an - gels watch -in' o - ver me.   All _____ night, all _____ day,
an - gels watch -in' o - ver me.

an - gels watch - in' o - ver me, my Lord. __ All _____ night,

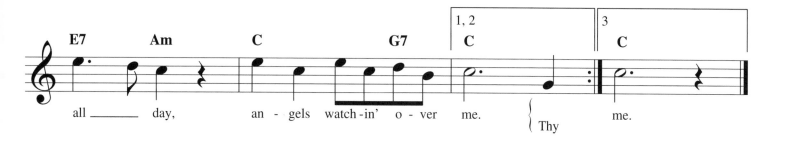

all _____ day, an - gels watch -in' o - ver me.
Thy   me.

ALL THROUGH THE NIGHT

Welsh Folksong

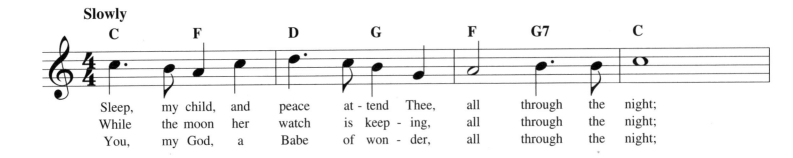

Sleep, my child, and peace at - tend Thee, all through the night;
While the moon her watch is keep - ing, all through the night;
You, my God, a Babe of won - der, all through the night;

guard - ian an - gels God will send Thee, all through the night.
while the wea - ry world is sleep - ing, all through the night.
dreams You dream can't break from thun - der, all through the night.

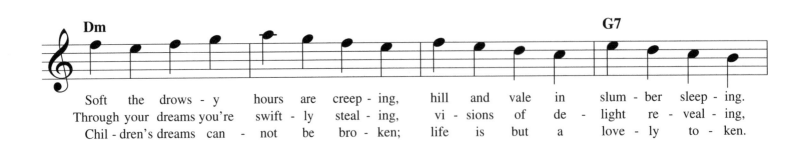

Soft the drows - y hours are creep - ing, hill and vale in slum - ber sleep - ing.
Through your dreams you're swift - ly steal - ing, vi - sions of de - light re - veal - ing,
Chil - dren's dreams can - not be bro - ken; life is but a love - ly to - ken.

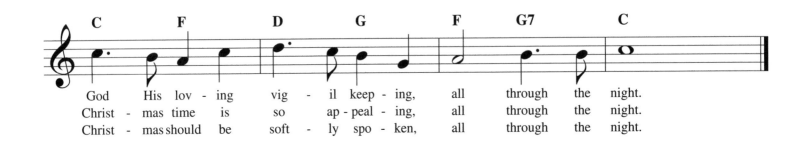

God His lov - ing vig - il keep - ing, all through the night.
Christ - mas time is so ap - peal - ing, all through the night.
Christ - mas should be soft - ly spo - ken, all through the night.

ALOHA OE

Words and Music by
QUEEN LILIUOKALANI

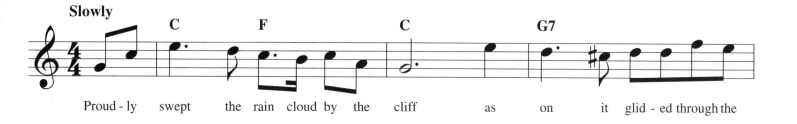

Proud - ly swept the rain cloud by the cliff as on it glid - ed through the

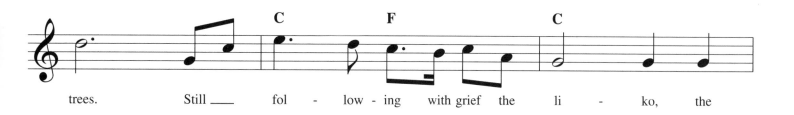

trees. Still ___ fol - low - ing with grief the li - ko, the

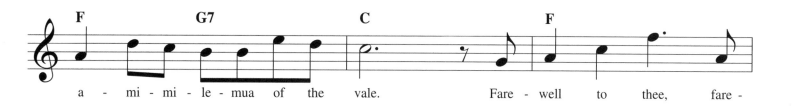

a - mi - mi - le - mua of the vale. Fare - well to thee, fare -

well to thee, thou charm - ing one who dwells a - mong the bow - ers. One

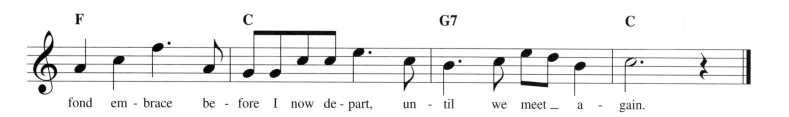

fond em - brace be - fore I now de - part, un - til we meet ___ a - gain.

ALOUETTE

Traditional

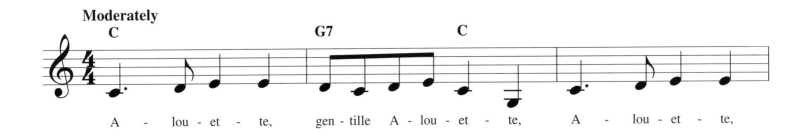

Moderately

A - lou - et - te, gen - tille A - lou - et - te, A - lou - et - te,

je te plu - me - rai.   Je te plu - me - rai

1. la tête,
2. le bec,
3. le nez
4. le dos,
5. les jambes,
6. les pieds
7. les pattes,
8. le cou,

Je te plu - me - rai

la tête,
le bec,
le nez
le dos,
les jambes,
les pieds
les pattes,
le cou,

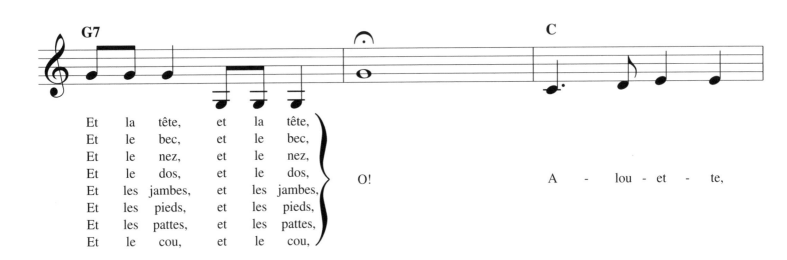

Et la tête, et la tête,
Et le bec, et le bec,
Et le nez, et le nez,
Et le dos, et le dos,
Et les jambes, et les jambes,
Et les pieds, et les pieds,
Et les pattes, et les pattes,
Et le cou, et le cou,

O!   A - lou - et - te,

gen - tille A - lou - et - te, A - lou - et - te, je te plu - me - rai.

AND THE GREEN GRASS GROWS ALL AROUND

Traditional

Brightly

1. There was a tree (there was a tree) all in the wood (all in the
2. tree (and on that tree) there was a limb (there was a
3. limb (and on that limb) there was a branch (there was a
4.-10. *(See addtional lyrics)*

wood,) the pret - ti - est tree (the pret - ti - est tree) that you ev - er did
limb,) the pret - ti - est limb (the pret - ti - est limb) that you ev - er did
branch,) the pret - ti - est branch (the pret - ti - est branch) that you ev - er did

see (that you ev - er did see.) Now the tree in a hole and the
see (that you ev - er did see.) Now the limb on the tree and the
see (that you ev - er did see.) Now the branch on the limb and the

Repeat as necessary

hole in the ground, and the green grass grows all a - round, all a - round, and the

green grass grows all a - round.

1–9
2.-4., 7.-10. And on that
5.,6. And in that
round.

10

Additional Lyrics

4. And on that branch there was a nest
The prettiest nest that you ever did see.
Now the nest on the branch...

5. And in that nest there was an egg
The prettiest egg that you ever did see.
Now the egg in the nest...

6. And in that egg there was a bird
The prettiest bird that you ever did see.
Now the bird in the egg...

7. And on that bird there was a wing
The prettiest wing that you ever did see.
Now the wing on the bird...

8. And on that wing there was a feather
The prettiest feather that you ever did see.
Now the feather on the wing...

9. And on that feather there was a bug
The prettiest bug that you ever did see.
Now the bug on the feather...

10. And on that bug there was a germ
The prettiest germ that you ever did see.
Now the germ on the bug...

ANIMAL FAIR

American Folksong

Lightly, in 2

I went to the an - i - mal fair, _____ the birds and beasts were

there. _____ The big ba - boon, by the light of the moon, was

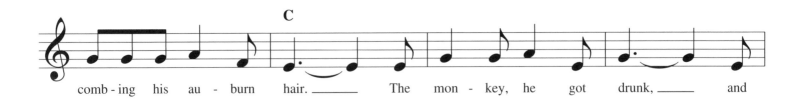

comb - ing his au - burn hair. _____ The mon - key, he got drunk, _____ and

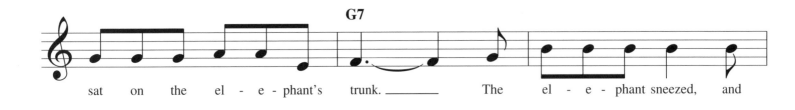

sat on the el - e - phant's trunk. _____ The el - e - phant sneezed, and

fell on his knees, and what be - came of the monk, the monk, the monk, the monk?

ARKANSAS TRAVELER

Southern American Folksong

Rhythmically

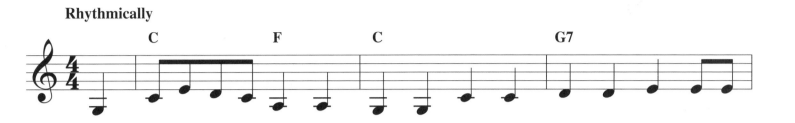

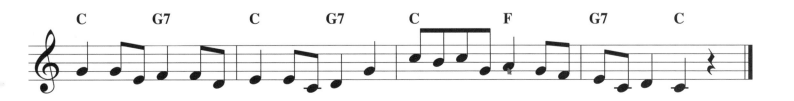

ANNABEL LEE

Traditional American Folksong

Flowing

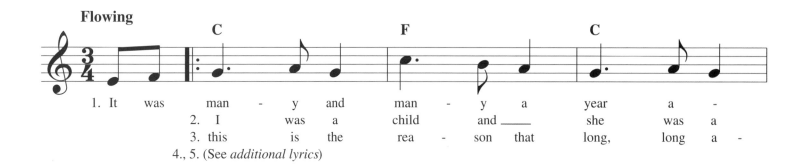

1. It was man - y and man - y a year a -
2. I was a child and ____ she was a
3. this is the rea - son that long, long a -
4., 5. (See *additional lyrics*)

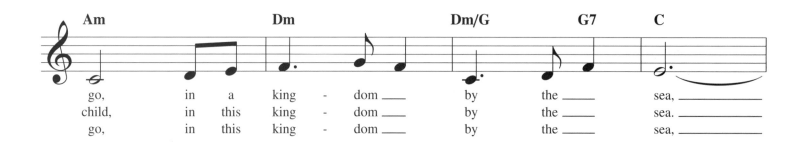

go, in a king - dom ____ by the ____ sea, ____
child, in this king - dom ____ by the ____ sea. ____
go, in this king - dom ____ by the ____ sea, ____

____ that a maid - en there lived whom you may know by
____ But we loved with a love that was great - er than
____ there a - rose a strong wind blow - ing out of a

name, by the name of ____ An - na - bel Lee. ____
love, so loved I and my An - na - bel Lee. ____
cloud, chilled and killed my dear An - na - bel Lee. ____

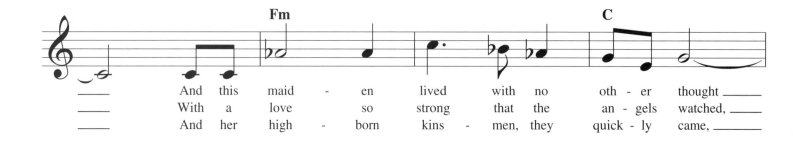

____ And this maid - en lived with no oth - er thought ____
____ With a love so strong that the an - gels watched, ____
____ And her high - born kins - men, they quick - ly came, ____

than to love and be loved by me. _____
e - ven cov - et - ed her and me. _____
and they bore her a - way from me. _____

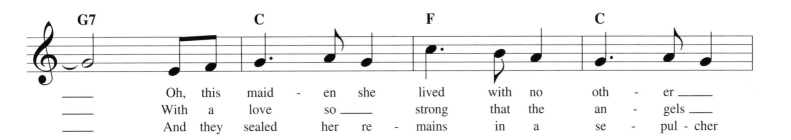

_____ Oh, this maid - en she lived with no oth - er _____
_____ With a love so _____ strong that the an - gels _____
_____ And they sealed her re - mains in a se - pul - cher

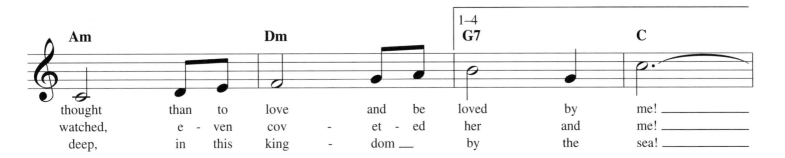

thought than to love and be loved by me! _____
watched, e - ven cov - et - ed her and me! _____
deep, in this king - dom _____ by the sea! _____

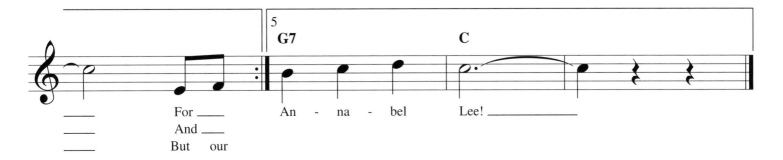

_____ For _____ An - na - bel Lee! _____
_____ And _____
_____ But our

Additional Lyrics

4. But our love, it was stronger by far than the love of the ones who were older than we,
   Of the many far older and wiser than we, of those older and wiser than we.
   Ah, but neither angel in the sky above, nor the demons beneath the sea,
   Could sever my soul from the soul of my love of my beautiful Annabel Lee!

5. And the moon never beams without bringing me dreams in this kingdom by the sea,
   And the stars never rise but I feel the bright eyes of the beautiful Annabel Lee.
   Through the night I lie by my dearest one, by the side of my bride to be,
   Though she lies in her sepulcher silent and cold, oh, my beautiful Annabel Lee!

THE ASH GROVE

Old Welsh Air

AULD LANG SYNE

Words by ROBERT BURNS
Traditional Scottish Melody

Slowly

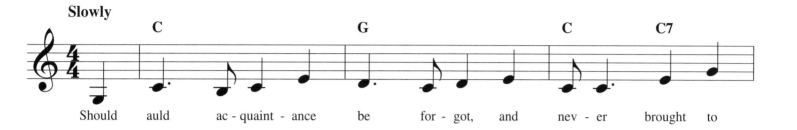

Should auld ac - quaint - ance be for - got, and nev - er brought to

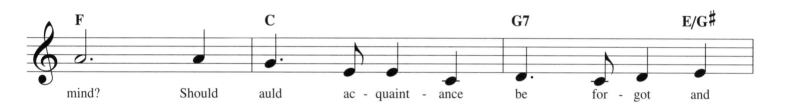

mind? Should auld ac - quaint - ance be for - got and

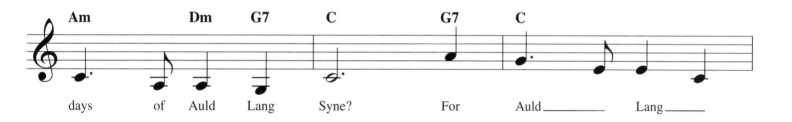

days of Auld Lang Syne? For Auld_____ Lang_____

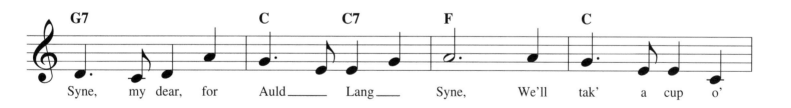

Syne, my dear, for Auld_____ Lang_____ Syne, We'll tak' a cup o'

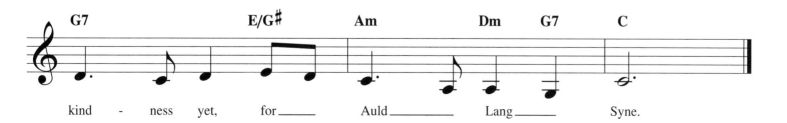

kind - ness yet, for_____ Auld_____ Lang_____ Syne.

AURA LEE

Words by W.W. FOSDICK
Music by GEORGE R. POULTON

Flowing

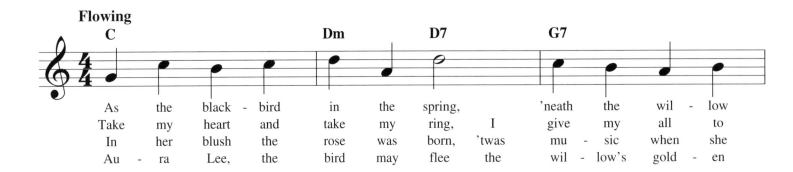

As the black - bird in the spring, 'neath the wil - low
Take my heart and take my ring, I give my all to
In her blush the rose was born, 'twas mu - sic when she
Au - ra Lee, the bird may flee the wil - low's gold - en

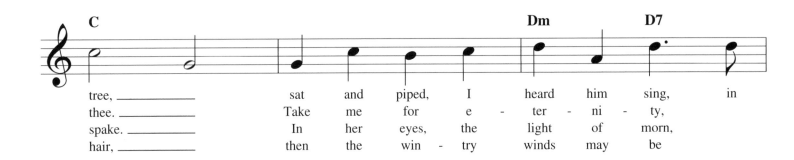

tree, _____ sat and piped, I heard him sing, in
thee. _____ Take me for e - ter - ni - ty,
spake. _____ In her eyes, the light of morn,
hair, _____ then the win - try winds may be

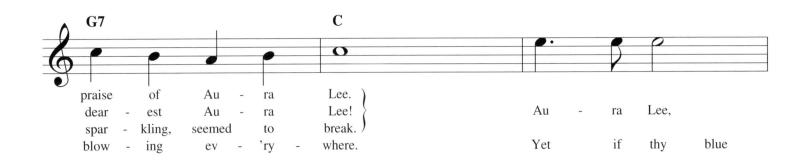

praise of Au - ra Lee.
dear - est Au - ra Lee!
spar - kling, seemed to break.
blow - ing ev - 'ry - where.

Au - ra Lee,
Yet if thy blue

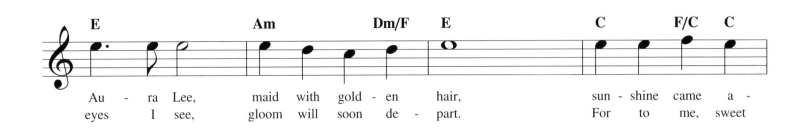

Au - ra Lee, maid with gold - en hair, sun - shine came a -
eyes I see, gloom will soon de - part. For to me, sweet

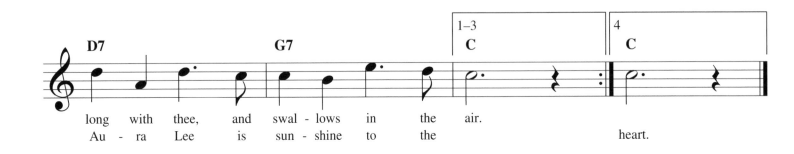

long with thee, and swal - lows in the air.
Au - ra Lee is sun - shine to the heart.

THE BAMBOO FLUTE

Chinese Folksong

Moderately

THE BALLAD OF NED KELLY

19th Century Australian

Lively

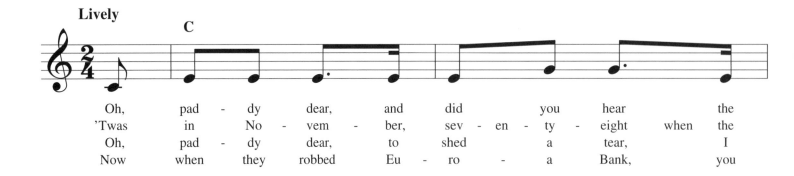

Oh, pad - dy dear, and did you hear the
'Twas in No - vem - ber, sev - en - ty - eight when the
Oh, pad - dy dear, to shed a tear, I
Now when they robbed Eu - ro - a Bank, you

news that's go - ing round? On the head of bold Ned
Kel - ly gang came down; just af - ter shoot - ing
can't but sym - pa - thize. Those Kel - lys are the
said they'd be run down. But now they've robbed an -

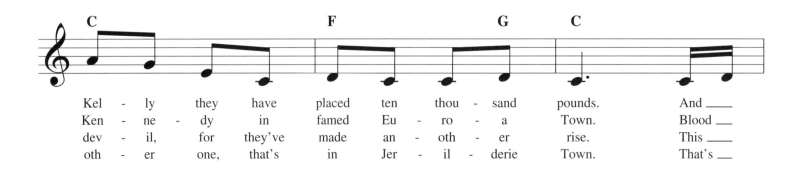

Kel - ly they have placed ten thou - sand pounds. And ____
Ken - ne - dy in famed Eu - ro - a Town. Blood ____
dev - il, for they've made an - oth - er rise. This ____
oth - er one, that's in Jer - il - derie Town. That's ____

on Joe Byrne, Steve Hart and Dan a thou - sand more they'd
hors - es they were all up - on, re - volv - ers in their
time a - cross the Bil - la - bong, where Mor - gan had his
in Jer - il - derie Town, me boys, and we're here to take their

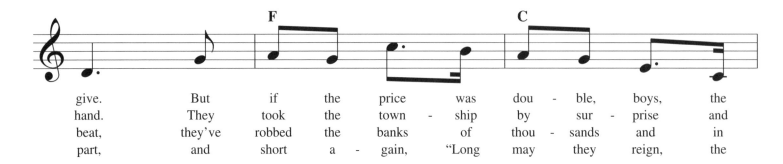

give. But if the price was dou - ble, boys, the
hand. They took the town - ship by sur - prise and
beat, they've robbed the banks of thou - sands and in
part, and short a - gain, "Long may they reign, the

THE BANANA BOAT SONG
(Day Oh)

Jamaican Work Song

Smoothly

Day   oh,   day ___ oh,   day da light ___ an' me

wan'   go home.   Come, Mis - ter Tal - ly - man, come tal - ly me ba - na - na.

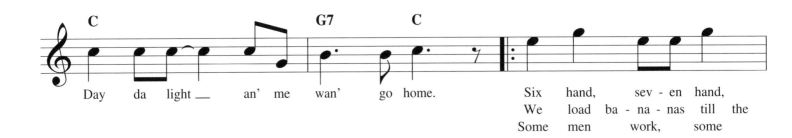

Day da light ___ an' me wan' go home.   Six   hand,   sev - en hand,
                                          We   load ba - na - nas till the
                                          Some men   work,   some

shout!   *shout!*

eight hand bunch!   Six   hand,   sev - en hand   eight   hand bunch!
ear - ly light.   Sleep   all   day   and   work all night.
men make love.   We   load ba - na - na while the moon a - bove.

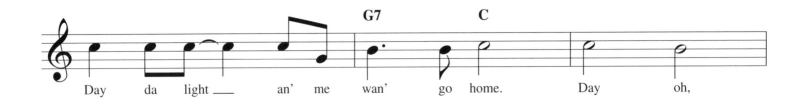

Day da light ___ an' me wan' go home.   Day   oh,

1, 2   3

day ___ oh,   day da light ___ an' me wan' go home.   wan' go home.

THE BAND PLAYED ON

Words by JOHN F. PALMER
Music by CHARLES B. WARD

BEAUTIFUL BROWN EYES

Traditional

BEAUTIFUL DREAMER

Words and Music by
STEPHEN C. FOSTER

BELIEVE ME, IF ALL THOSE ENDEARING YOUNG CHARMS

Words and Music by
THOMAS MOORE

Broadly

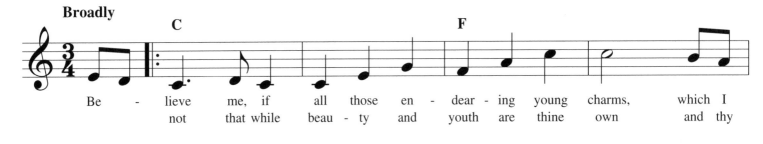

Be - lieve me, if all those en - dear - ing young charms, which I
not that while beau - ty and youth are thine own and thy

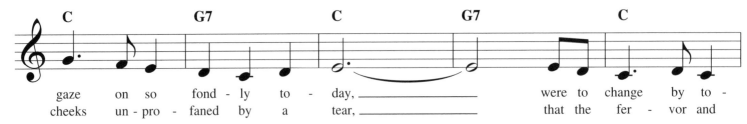

gaze on so fond - ly to - day, _____ were to change by to -
cheeks un - pro - faned by a tear, _____ that the fer - vor and

mor - row and fleet in my arms like the fair - y gifts fad - ing a -
faith of a soul can be known to which time will but make thee more

way, _____ thou wouldst still be a - dored as this
dear. _____ No, the heart that has tru - ly loved

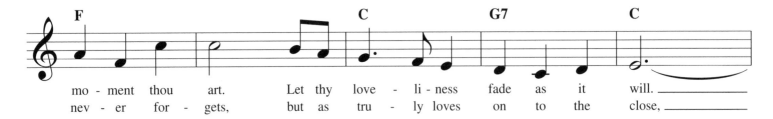

mo - ment thou art. Let thy love - li - ness fade as it will. _____
nev - er for - gets, but as tru - ly loves on to the close, _____

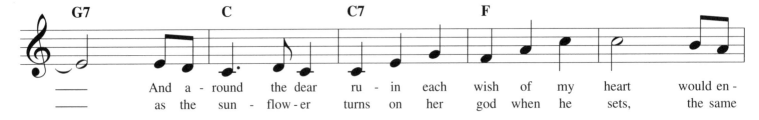

_____ And a - round the dear ru - in each wish of my heart would en -
_____ as the sun - flow - er turns on her god when he sets, the same

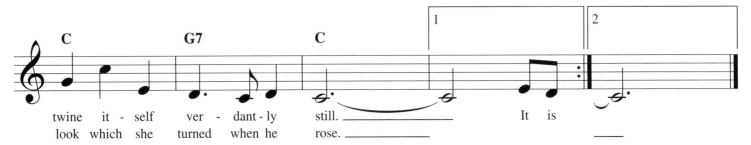

twine it - self ver - dant - ly still. _____ It is
look which she turned when he rose. _____

BLOW THE MAN DOWN

Traditional Sea Chantey

Moderately, in 1

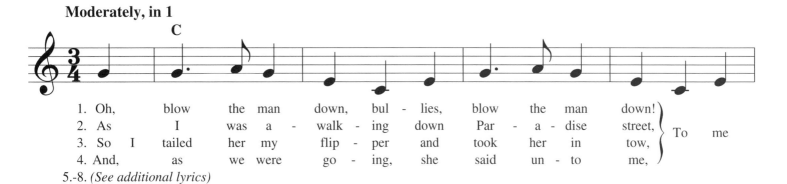

1. Oh, blow the man down, bul - lies, blow the man down!
2. As I was a - walk - ing down Par - a - dise street,
3. So I tailed her my flip - per and took her in tow,
4. And, as we were go - ing, she said un - to me,

5.-8. (*See additional lyrics*)

To me

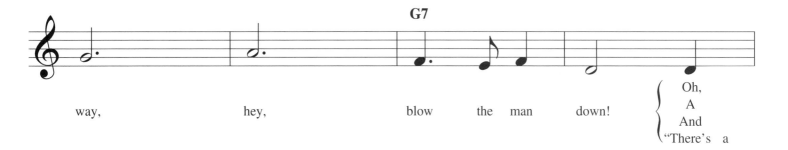

way, hey, blow the man down!

Oh,
A
And
"There's a

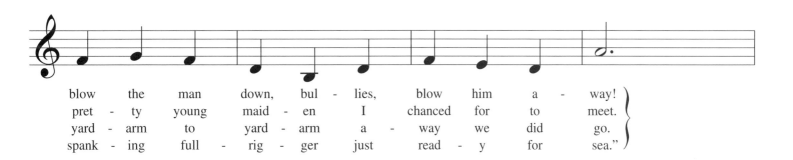

blow the man down, bul - lies, blow him a - way!
pret - ty young maid - en I chanced for to meet.
yard - arm to yard - arm a - way we did go.
spank - ing full - rig - ger just read - y for sea."

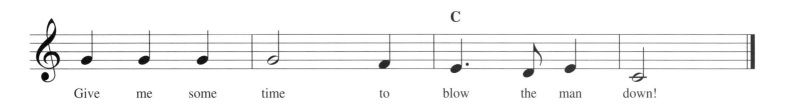

Give me some time to blow the man down!

Additional Lyrics

5. The spanking fullrigger for New York was bound,
   To me way, hey, blow the man down.
   She was very well manned, she was very well found,
   Give me some time to blow the man down!

6. But as soon as that packet was clear of the bar,
   To me way, hey, blow the man down.
   The mate knocked me down with the end of a spar,
   Give me some time to blow the man down!

7. And as soon as that packet was out on the sea,
   To me way, hey, blow the man down.
   'Twas dev'lish hard treatment of ev'ry degree,
   Give me some time to blow the man down!

8. So I give you fair warning before we belay;
   To me way, hey, blow the man down.
   Don't never take heed of what pretty girls say,
   Give me some time to blow the man down!

THE BLUE BELLS OF SCOTLAND

Words and Music attributed to
MRS. JORDON

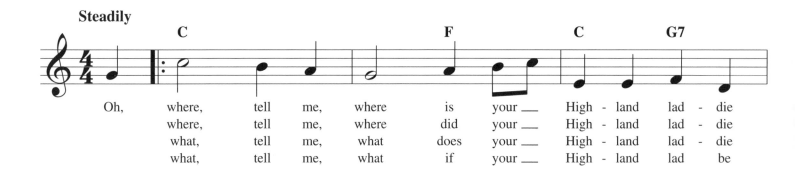

Oh, where, tell me, where is your __ High - land lad - die
where, tell me, where did your __ High - land lad - die
what, tell me, what does your __ High - land lad - die
what, tell me, what if your __ High - land lad be

gone? Oh, where, tell me, where is your __ High - land lad - die
dwell? Oh, where, tell me, where did your __ High - land lad - die
wear? Oh, what, tell me, what does your __ High - land lad - die
slain? Oh, what, tell me, what if your __ High - land lad be

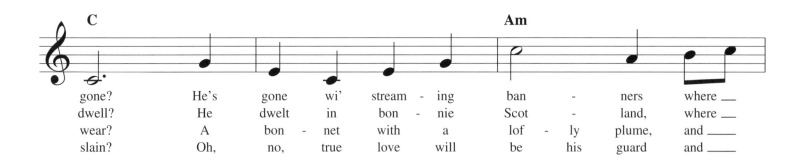

gone? He's gone wi' stream - ing ban - ners where __
dwell? He dwelt in bon - nie Scot - land, where __
wear? A bon - net with a lof - ly plume, and __
slain? Oh, no, true love will be his guard and __

no - ble deeds are done. And it's, oh, in my
blooms the sweet blue bell. And it's, oh, in my
on his breast a plaid. And it's, oh, in my
bring him safe a - gain. For it's, oh, my heart would

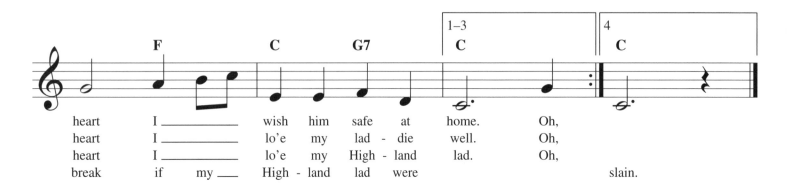

heart I __ wish him safe at home. Oh,
heart I __ lo'e my lad - die well. Oh,
heart I __ lo'e my High - land lad. Oh,
break if my __ High - land lad were slain.

THE BLUE TAIL FLY
(Jimmy Crack Corn)

Words and Music by
DANIEL DECATUR EMMETT

Lively

1. When I was young, I used to wait on mas - ter, hand - ing him his plate. I
2. He used to ride each af - ter - noon, I'd fol - low with a hick - 'ry broom. The
3. The po - ny jump, he run, he pitch, he threw my mas - ter in the ditch. My
4.,5. *(See additional lyrics)*

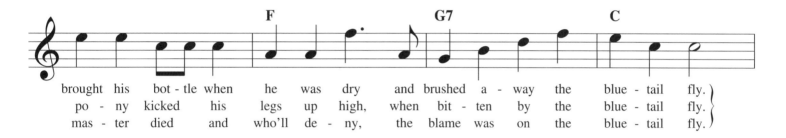

brought his bot - tle when he was dry and brushed a - way the blue - tail fly.
po - ny kicked his legs up high, when bit - ten by the blue - tail fly.
mas - ter died and who'll de - ny, the blame was on the blue - tail fly.

Chorus

Jim - my crack corn and I don't care, Jim - my crack corn and I don't care,

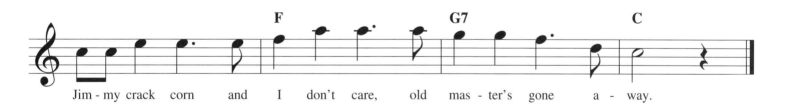

Jim - my crack corn and I don't care, old mas - ter's gone a - way.

Additional Lyrics

4. Old master's dead and gone to rest,
   They say it happened for the best.
   I won't forget until I die
   My master and the blue-tail fly.
   Chorus

5. A skeeter bites right through your clothes,
   A hornet strikes you on the nose,
   The bees may get you passing by,
   But, oh, much worse, the blue-tail fly.
   Chorus

BOTANY BAY

Australian Folksong

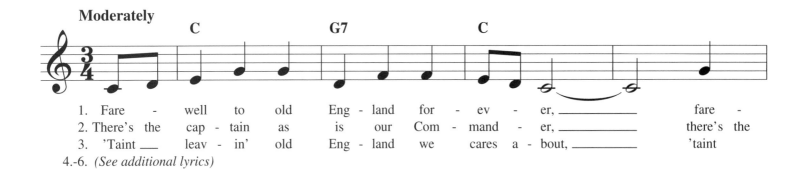

1. Fare - well to old Eng - land for - ev - er, _____ fare -
2. There's the cap - tain as is our Com - mand - er, _____ there's the
3. 'Taint ___ leav - in' old Eng - land we cares a - bout, _____ 'taint

4.-6. *(See additional lyrics)*

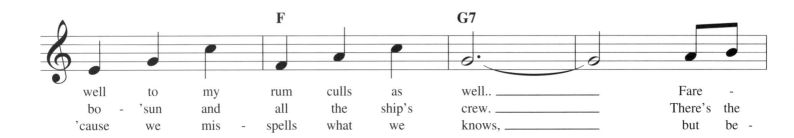

well to my rum culls as well.. _____ Fare -
bo - 'sun and all the ship's crew. _____ There's the
'cause we mis - spells what we knows, _____ but be -

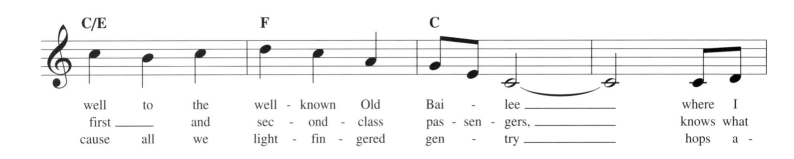

well to the well - known Old Bai - lee _____ where I
first _____ and sec - ond - class pas - sen - gers, _____ knows what
cause all we light - fin - gered gen - try _____ hops a -

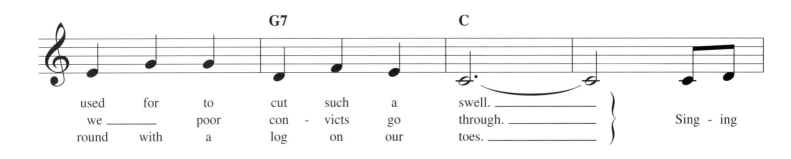

used for to cut such a swell. _____ Sing - ing
we _____ poor con - victs go through. _____
round with a log on our toes. _____

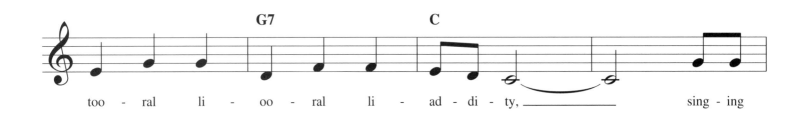

too - ral li - oo - ral li - ad - di - ty, _____ sing - ing

too - ral li - oo - ral li - ay. _____ Sing - ing

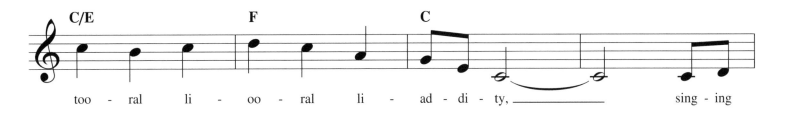

too - ral li - oo - ral li - ad - di - ty, _____ sing - ing

too - ral li - oo - ral li - ay. _____

Additional Lyrics

4. For seven long years I'll be staying here,
   For seven long years and a day.
   For meeting a cove in an area
   And taking his ticker away.

5. Oh, had I the wings of a turtledove!
   I'd soar on my pinions so high.
   Slap bang to the arms of my Polly love,
   And in her sweet presence I'd die.

6. Now, all my young Dookies and Duchesses,
   Take warning from what I've to say.
   Mind all is your own as you touchesses,
   Or you'll find us in Botany Bay.

BUFFALO GALS
(Won't You Come Out Tonight?)

Words and Music by
COOL WHITE (JOHN HODGES)

With motion

Buf - fa - lo gals, won't ya come out to - night, won't ya come out to - night, won't ya
Yes, pret - ty boys, we'll come out to - night, we'll come out to - night, we'll

come out to - night? Buf - fa - lo gals, won't ya come out to - night and
come out to - night. Yes, pret - ty boys, we'll come out to - night and

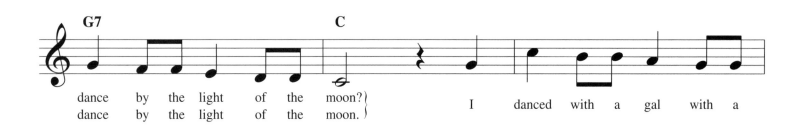

dance by the light of the moon? I danced with a gal with a
dance by the light of the moon.

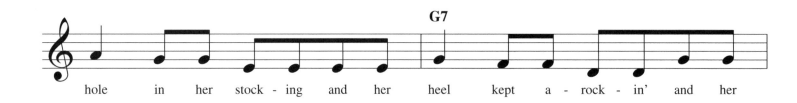

hole in her stock - ing and her heel kept a - rock - in' and her

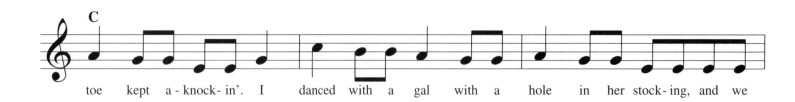

toe kept a - knock - in'. I danced with a gal with a hole in her stock - ing, and we

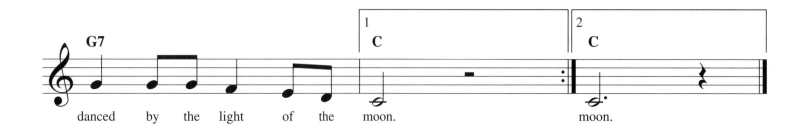

danced by the light of the moon.   moon.

CAMPTOWN RACES

Words and Music by
STEPHEN C. FOSTER

CARRY ME BACK TO OLD VIRGINNY

Words and Music by
JAMES A. BLAND

Car - ry   me back   to   old   Vir - gin - ny,   there's where the   cot - ton and the
Car - ry   me back   to   old   Vir - gin - ny,   there   let   me   live ___ till   I

corn and 'ta - ters grow.   There's where the   birds   war - ble   sweet   in   the spring-time,
with - er   and   de - cay.   Long   by   the   old,   dis - mal swamp have   I   wan - dered,

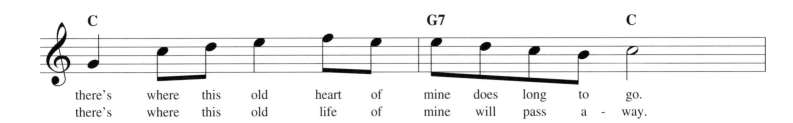

there's where   this   old   heart   of   mine does   long   to   go.
there's where   this   old   life   of   mine will   pass   a - way.

There's where   I   la - bored so   hard   for   my fa - ther,   day   af - ter day   in   the
Fa - ther and moth - er have   long   gone be - fore me,   soon   we will meet   on   that

field   of yel - low corn.   No   place on earth   do   I   love   more sin - cere - ly
bright and gold - en shore.   There we'll be   hap - py and   free   from   all sor - row,

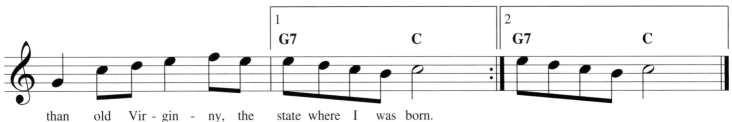

than   old   Vir - gin - ny, the   state where I   was born.
there's where we'll meet   and we'll   nev - er part   no more.

CHIAPANECAS

Mexican Folksong

CASEY JONES

Words by T. LAWRENCE SEIBERT
Music by EDDIE NEWTON

CIELITO LINDO
(My Pretty Darling)

By C. FERNANDEZ

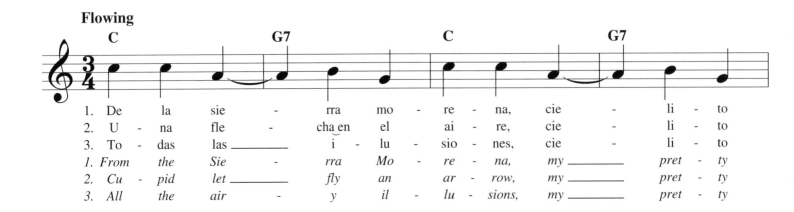

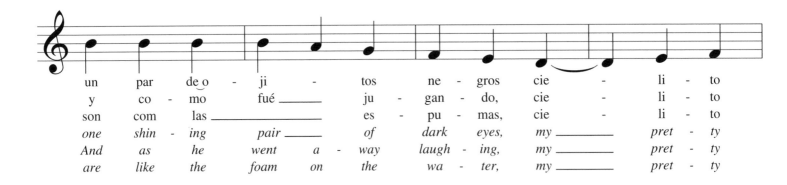

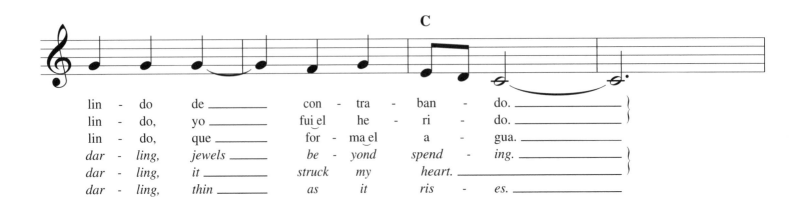

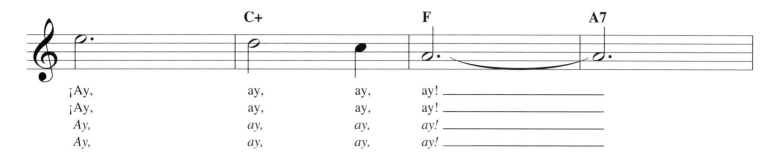

¡Ay, ay, ay, ay! _____
¡Ay, ay, ay, ay! _____
Ay, ay, ay, ay! _____
Ay, ay, ay, ay! _____

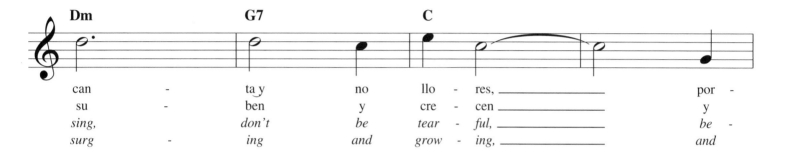

can - ta y no llo - res, _____ por -
su - ben y cre - cen _____ y
sing, don't be tear - ful, _____ *be -*
surg - ing and grow - ing, _____ *and*

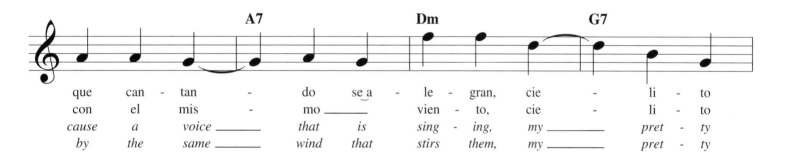

que can - tan - do se a - le - gran, cie - li - to
con el mis - mo vien - to, cie - li - to
cause a voice _____ that is sing - ing, my _____ pret - ty
by the same _____ wind that stirs them, my _____ pret - ty

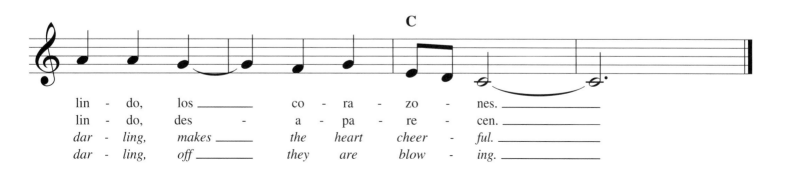

lin - do, los _____ co - ra - zo - nes. _____
lin - do, des - a - pa - re - cen. _____
dar - ling, makes _____ the heart cheer - ful. _____
dar - ling, off _____ they are blow - ing. _____

CINDY

Southern Appalachian Folksong

Quickly

C

1. You ought to see my Cin - dy, she lives a - way down
2. I wish I was an ap - ple a - hang - in' on a
3. I wish I had a nee - dle as fine as I could
4., 5. *(See additional lyrics)*

G7 **C7** **F** **G7**

south, and she's so sweet the hon - ey - bees ___ swarm a - round her
tree, and ev - 'ry time my Cin - dy passed she'd take a bite of
sew, I'd sew that gal to my coat - tail, and down the road I'd

C **F**

mouth.
me. } Get a - long home, Cin - dy, Cin - dy, get a - long
go.

C **F**

home, Cin - dy, Cin - dy, get a - long home, Cin - dy,

G7 **C**

Cin - dy, I'll mar - ry you some - day.

Additional Lyrics

4. I wish I had a nickel,
   I wish I had a dime,
   I wish I had my Cindy girl
   To love me all the time.

5. Cindy in the springtime,
   Cindy in the fall;
   If I can't have my Cindy,
   I'll have no girl at all.

(Oh, My Darling)
CLEMENTINE

Words and Music by
PERCY MONTROSE

Moderately

In a cav - ern, in a can - yon, ex - ca - vat - ing for a
was, and like a fair - y, and her shoes were num - ber
duck - lings to the wa - ter ev - 'ry morn - ing just at
lips a - bove the wa - ter, blow - ing bub - bles soft and

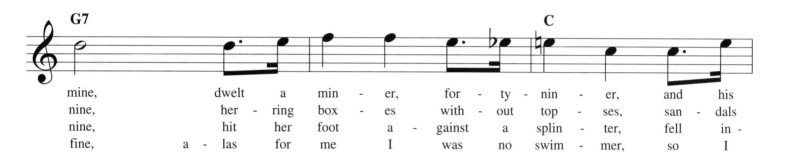

mine, dwelt a min - er, for - ty - nin - er, and his
nine, her - ring box - es with - out top - ses, san - dals
nine, hit her foot a - gainst a splin - ter, fell in -
fine, a - las for me I was no swim - mer, so I

daugh - ter, Clem - en - tine.
were for Clem - en - tine.
to the foam - ing brine.
lost my Clem - en - tine.

Oh, my dar - ling, oh, my

dar - ling, oh, my dar - ling, Clem - en - tine, you are lost and gone for-

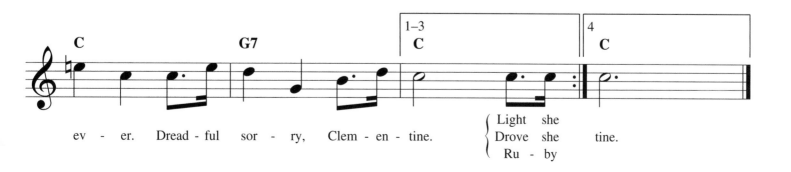

ev - er. Dread - ful sor - ry, Clem - en - tine.

1–3
Light she
Drove she tine.
Ru - by

COCKLES AND MUSSELS
(Molly Malone)

Traditional Irish Folksong

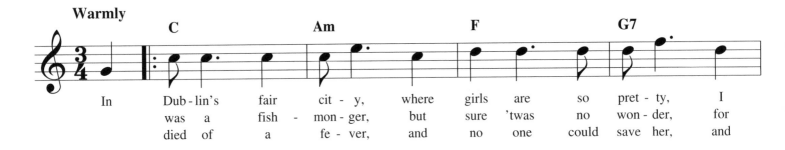

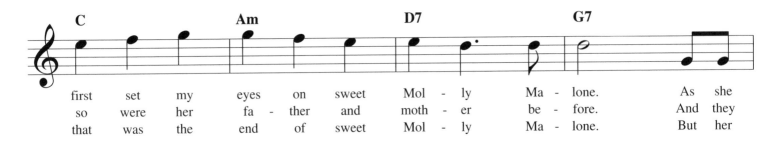

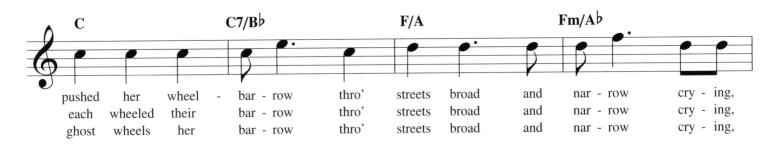

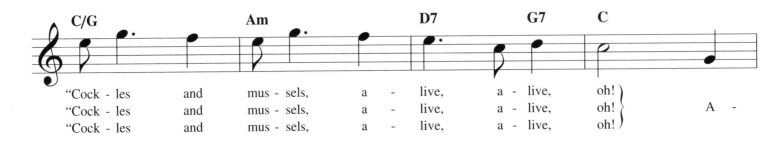

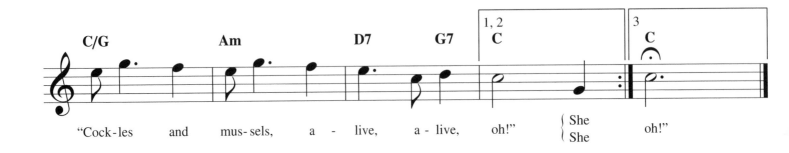

COUNTRY GARDENS

Traditional

DANNY BOY
(Londonderry Air)

Words by FREDERICK EDWARD WEATHERLY
Traditional Irish Folk Melody

Slowly

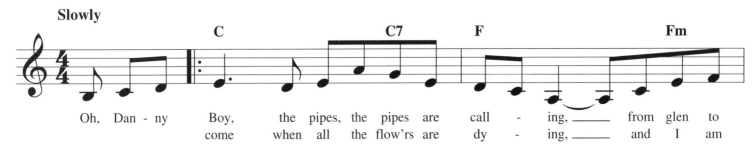

Oh, Dan - ny Boy, the pipes, the pipes are call - ing, _____ from glen to
come when all the flow'rs are dy - ing, _____ and I am

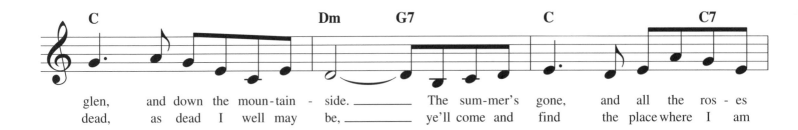

glen, and down the moun - tain - side. _____ The sum - mer's gone, and all the ros - es
dead, as dead I well may be, _____ ye'll come and find the place where I am

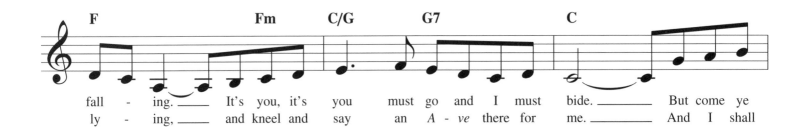

fall - ing. _____ It's you, it's you must go and I must bide. _____ But come ye
ly - ing, _____ and kneel and say an *A - ve* there for me. _____ And I shall

back when sum - mer's in the mead - ow, _____ or when the val - ley's hush'd and white with
hear, tho' soft, your tread a - bove _ me, _____ and all my dreams will warm and sweet - er

snow. _____ 'Tis I'll be there in sun - shine or in shad - ow, _____ oh, Dan - ny
be. _____ If you will not fail to tell me that you love _ me, _____ then I shall

Boy, oh, Dan - ny Boy, I love you so! But if ye
sleep in peace un - til you come to me.

DOWN IN THE VALLEY

Traditional American Folksong

Moderately

Down in the val - ley, val - ley so
Ros - es love sun - shine, vi - 'lets so love
Write me a let - ter, send it by

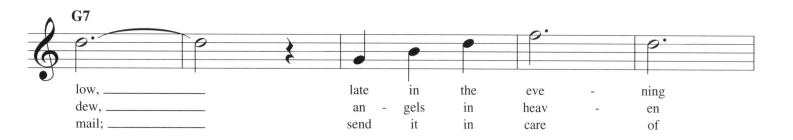

low, _____ late in the eve - ning
dew, _____ an - gels in heav - en
mail; _____ send it in care of

hear the train blow. _____ Hear that train blow -
know I love you. _____ Know I love you,
Bir - ming - ham jail. _____ Bir - ming - ham jail -

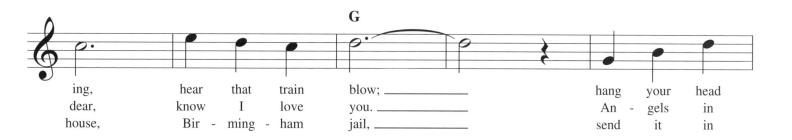

ing, hear that train blow; _____ hang your head
dear, know I love you. _____ An - gels in
house, Bir - ming - ham jail, _____ send it in

o - ver hear that train blow. _____
heav - en know I love you. _____
care of Bir - ming - ham jail. _____

DEEP RIVER

African-American Spiritual
Based on Joshua 3

Moderately

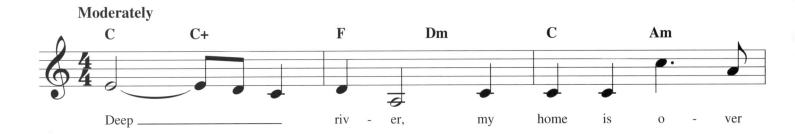

Deep _____ riv - er, my home is o - ver

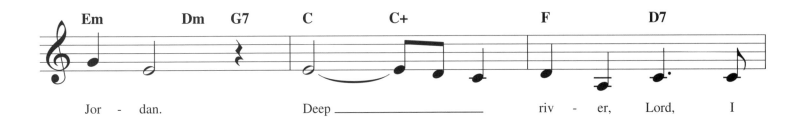

Jor - dan. Deep _____ riv - er, Lord, I

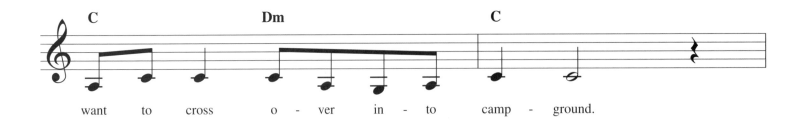

want to cross o - ver in - to camp - ground.

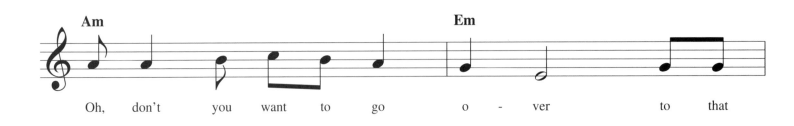

Oh, don't you want to go o - ver to that

gos - pel _____ feast, _____ that prom - ised

land _____ where all _____ is peace? Oh,

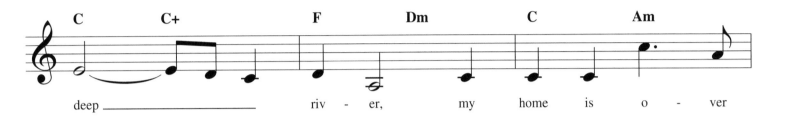

deep _____ riv - er, my home is o - ver

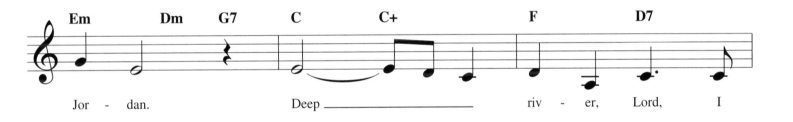

Jor - dan. Deep _____ riv - er, Lord, I

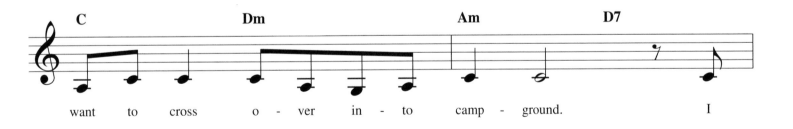

want to cross o - ver in - to camp - ground. I

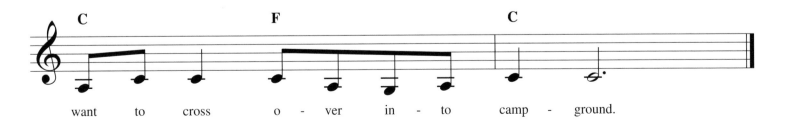

want to cross o - ver in - to camp - ground.

(I Wish I Was In)
DIXIE

Words and Music by
DANIEL DECATUR EMMETT

Brightly

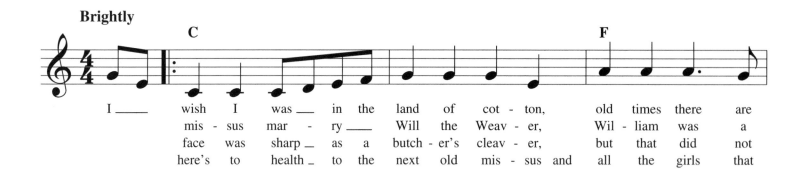

I ___ wish I was ___ in the land of cot - ton, old times there are
mis - sus mar - ry ___ Will the Weav - er, Wil - liam was a
face was sharp ___ as a butch - er's cleav - er, but that did not
here's to health ___ to the next old mis - sus and all the girls that

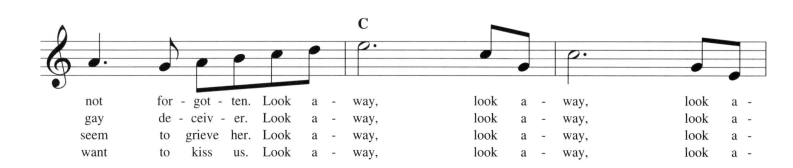

not for - got - ten. Look a - way, look a - way, look a -
gay de - ceiv - er. Look a - way, look a - way, look a -
seem to grieve her. Look a - way, look a - way, look a -
want to kiss us. Look a - way, look a - way, look a -

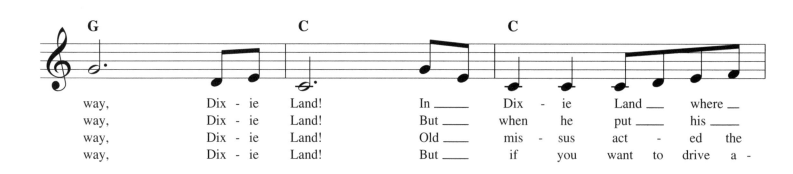

way, Dix - ie Land! In ___ Dix - ie Land ___ where ___
way, Dix - ie Land! But ___ when he put ___ his ___
way, Dix - ie Land! Old ___ mis - sus act - ed the
way, Dix - ie Land! But ___ if you want to drive a -

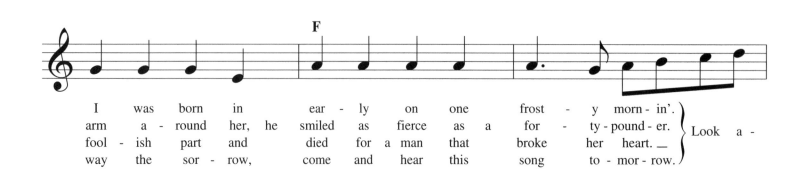

I was born in ear - ly on one frost - y morn - in'.
arm a - round her, he smiled as fierce as a for - ty-pound-er.
fool - ish part and died for a man that broke her heart. ___
way the sor - row, come and hear this song to - mor - row.
Look a -

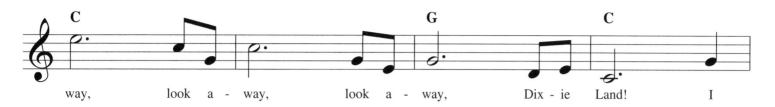

way,   look a - way,   look a - way,   Dix - ie   Land!   I

wish   I   was   in   Dix — ie.   Hoo — ray!   Hoo -

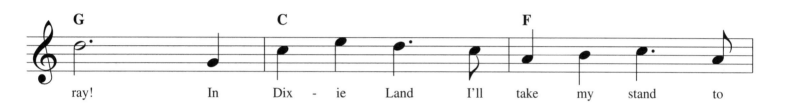

ray!   In   Dix — ie   Land   I'll   take   my   stand   to

live   and   die   in   Dix — ie.   A — way,   a — way,   a -

way   down   south   in   Dix — ie.   A — way,   a — way,   a -

way   down   south   in   Dix — ie.   Old ___ / His ___ / Now ___   Dix — ie.

DOWN BY THE RIVERSIDE

African-American Spiritual

Rhythmically

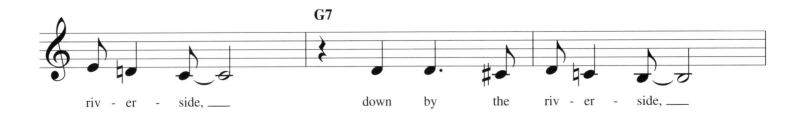

I ain't gon - na stud - y war ___ no more. Ain't gon - na

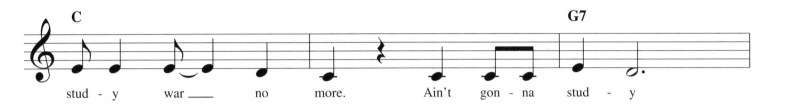

stud - y war ___ no more. Ain't gon - na stud - y

war no more. I ain't gon - na

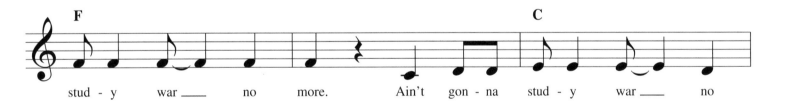

stud - y war ___ no more. Ain't gon - na stud - y war ___ no

more. Ain't gon - na stud - y _____ war no

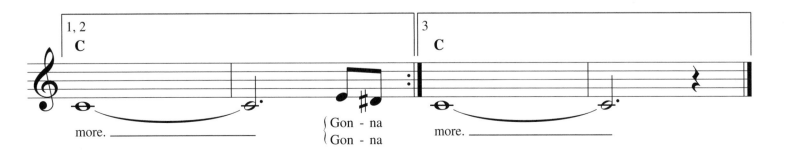

more. _____ Gon - na / Gon - na   more. _____

DRINK TO ME ONLY WITH THINE EYES

Lyrics by BEN JONSON
Traditional Music

THE DRUNKEN SAILOR

19th Century American Sea Chantey

Moderately

'Way hay, 'n' up she ris - es! Pat - ent blocks o' dif - f'rent siz - es,

'Way hay, 'n' up she ris - es, ear - lye in the morn - in'!

1. What shall we do wi' a drunk - en sail - or? What shall we do wi' a drunk - en sail - or?
2. Put him in the long - boat till he gets so - ber, put him in the long - boat till he gets so - ber,
3. Keep him __ there an' __ make him bail her, keep him __ there an' __ make him bail her,
4. Trice him __ up in a run - nin' bow - line, trice him __ up in a run - nin' bow - line,

5.-9. *(See additional lyrics)*

What shall we do wi' a drunk - en sail - or, ear - lye in the morn - in'?
put him in the long - boat till he gets so - ber, ear - lye in the morn - in'!
keep him __ there an' __ make him bail her, ear - lye in the morn - in'!
trice him __ up in a run - nin' bow - line, ear - lye in the morn - in'!

Additional Lyrics

5. Tie him to the taff-rail when she's yard-arm under,
   Earlye in the mornin'!

6. Put him in the scuppers with a hosepipe on him,
   Earlye in the mornin'!

7. Take him an' shake 'im, an' try an' wake 'im,
   Earlye in the mornin'!

8. Give him a dose o' salt an' water,
   Earlye in the mornin'!

9. Give him a taste o' the bosun's rope-end,
   Earlye in the mornin'!

DU, DU LIEGST MIR IM HERZEN
(You, You Weigh on My Heart)

German Folksong

FLOW GENTLY, SWEET AFTON

Lyrics by ROBERT BURNS
Music by ALEXANDER HUME

THE ERIE CANAL

New York Work Song, circa 1820

Moderately

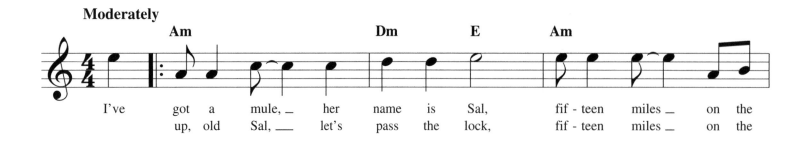

I've got a mule, _ her name is Sal, fif - teen miles _ on the
up, old Sal, _ let's pass the lock, fif - teen miles _ on the

E - rie Ca - nal. ___ She's a good hard work - er and a
E - rie Ca - nal, ___ in Sche - nec - ta - dy ___ to - day at

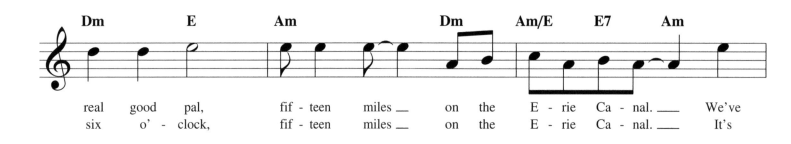

real good pal, fif - teen miles _ on the E - rie Ca - nal. __ We've
six o' - clock, fif - teen miles _ on the E - rie Ca - nal. __ It's

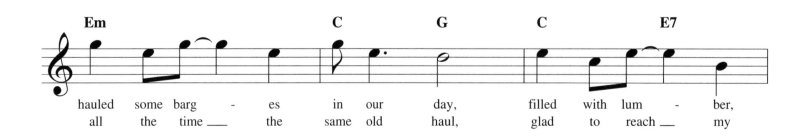

hauled some barg - es in our day, filled with lum - ber,
all the time _ the same old haul, glad to reach _ my

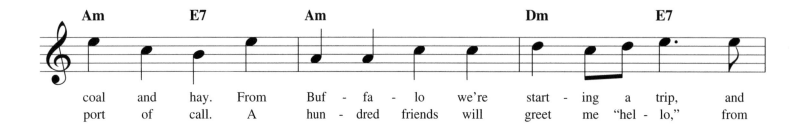

coal and hay. From Buf - fa - lo we're start - ing a trip, and
port of call. A hun - dred friends will greet me "hel - lo," from

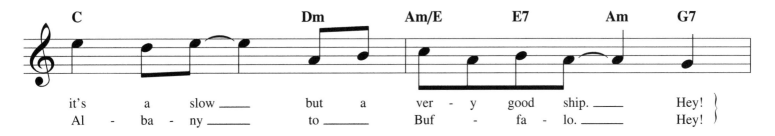

it's a slow ____ but a ver - y good ship. ____ Hey!
Al - ba - ny ____ to ____ Buf - fa - lo. ____ Hey!

Low bridge, ev - 'ry - bod - y down! Low bridge, we're a -

com - in' to a town! And you'll al - ways know your neigh - bor, you'll

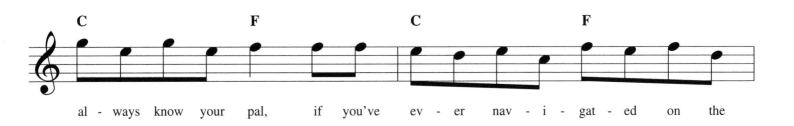

al - ways know your pal, if you've ev - er nav - i - gat - ed on the

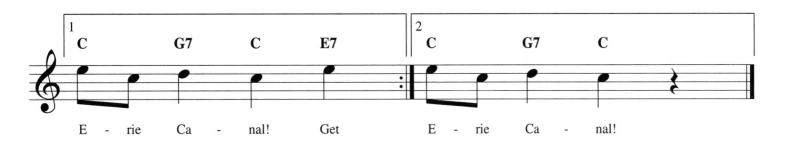

1
E - rie Ca - nal! Get

2
E - rie Ca - nal!

THE FOGGY, FOGGY DEW

Traditional

FOR HE'S A JOLLY GOOD FELLOW

Traditional

FRANKIE AND JOHNNY

Anonymous Blues Ballad

With motion

1. Frank-ie and John-ny were lov-ers, said they were real-ly in
2. Frank-ie and John-ny went walk-ing, John-ny had on ___ a new
3. John-ny said, "I've ___ got to leave now, but I won't be ___ ver-y
4.-6. *(See additional lyrics)*

love. Now Frank-ie was true ___ to her John-ny, true as
suit that Frank-ie had bought ___ with a "c - note," 'cause it
long. Don't sit up and wait ___ for me, hon-ey; don't you

all the stars a - bove. ⎫
made him look so cute. ⎬ He was her man, _____
wor - ry while I'm gone." ⎭

___ but he done her wrong. _____

Additional Lyrics

4. Frankie went down to the hotel,
   Looked in the window so high;
   There she saw her lovin' Johnny
   Making love to Nellie Bly.
   He was her man, but he done her wrong.

5. Johnny saw Frankie a-comin';
   Down the back stairs he did scoot.
   Frankie she took out her pistol;
   Oh, that lady sure could shoot!
   He was her man, but he done her wrong.

6. Frankie, she went to the big chair,
   Calm as a lady could be.
   Turning her eyes up, she whispered,
   "Lord, I'm coming up to Thee.
   He was my man, but he done me wrong."

FRÈRE JACQUES
(Are You Sleeping?)

Traditional

Broadly

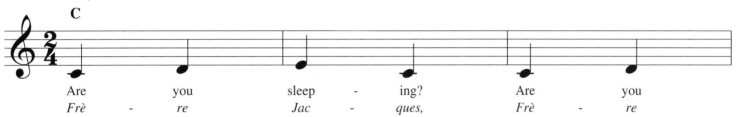

Are you sleep - ing? Are you
Frè - re Jac - ques, Frè - re

sleep - ing? Broth - er John, Broth - er
Jac - ques, Dor - mez vous? Dor - mez

John, morn - ing bells are ring - ing,
vous? son - nez les ma - ti - nes,

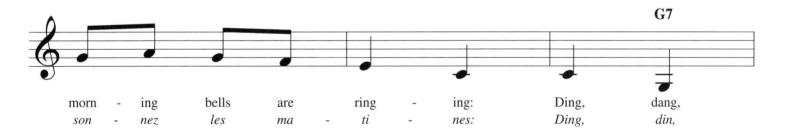

morn - ing bells are ring - ing: Ding, dang,
son - nez les ma - ti - nes: Ding, din,

dong! Ding, dang, dong!
don! Ding, din, don!

FUNICULI, FUNICULA

Words and Music by
LUIGI DENZA

Some think _____ the world is made for fun and
me! _____ 'Tis strange is that some should take and to

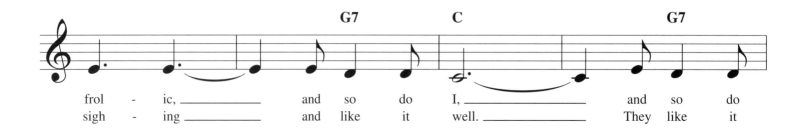

frol - ic, _____ and so do I, _____ and so do
sigh - ing _____ and like it well. _____ They like it

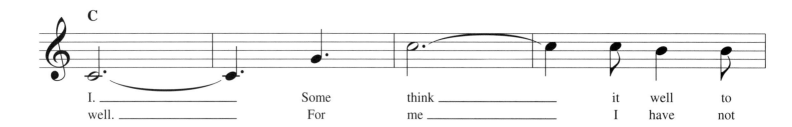

I. _____ Some think _____ it well to
well. _____ For me _____ I have not

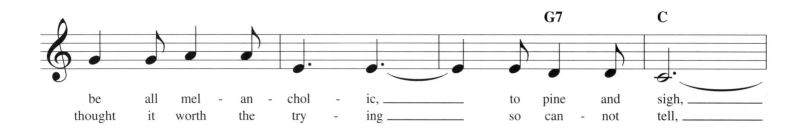

be all mel - an - chol - ic, _____ to pine and sigh, _____
thought it worth the try - ing _____ so can - not tell, _____

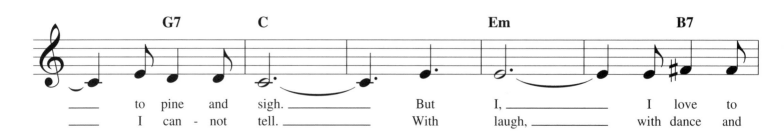

_____ to pine and sigh. _____ But I, _____ I love to
_____ I can - not tell. _____ With laugh, _____ with dance and

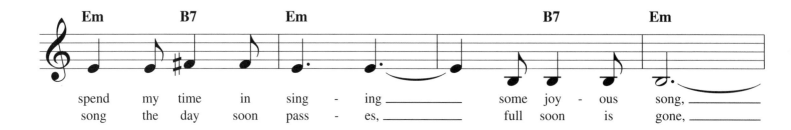

spend my time in sing - ing _____ some joy - ous song, _____
song the day soon pass - es, _____ full soon is gone, _____

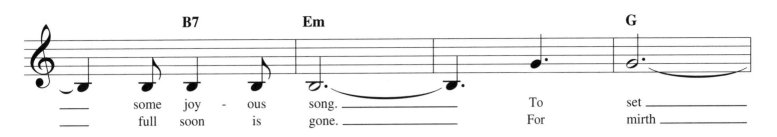

some joy - ous song. _____ To set _____
full soon is gone. _____ For mirth _____

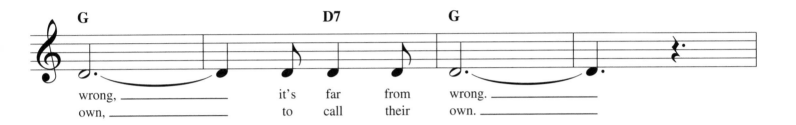

the air with mu - sic brave - ly ring - ing _____ is far from
was made for joy - ous lads and lass - es _____ to call their

wrong, _____ it's far from wrong. _____
own, _____ to call their own. _____

Lis - ten, lis - ten, mu - sic sounds a - far.
Lis - ten, lis - ten, hark the soft gui - tar.

Lis - ten, lis - ten, ech - oes sound a - far. Fu - ni - cu -

lì, fu - ni - cu - là, fu - ni - cu - lì, fu - ni - cu - là.

Joy is ev - 'ry - where, fu - ni - cu - lì, fu - ni - cu - là. Ah là.

THE GIRL I LEFT BEHIND ME

19th Century Irish

Moderately

1. The ___ hour was sad I left the maid, a lin - g'ring fare - well ___
2. Then ___ to the East we bore a - way to win a name ___ in ___
3. Full ___ man - y a name our ban - ners bore of for - mer deeds ___ of ___
4.,5. *(See additional lyrics)*

tak - ing, her ___ sighs and tears my steps de - layed. I
sto - ry, and ___ there, where dawns the sun of day, there
dar - ing, but ___ they were of the days of yore, in

thought her heart was ___ break - ing. In ___ hur - ried words her
dawned our sun of ___ glo - ry. Both ___ blazed in noon on
which we had no ___ shar - ing. But ___ now our lau - rels

name I blessed. I breathed the vows that bind me, and ___
Al - ma's heights when, in the past as - signed me, I ___
fresh - ly won with the old ones shall en - twined be, still ___

to my heart in an - guish pressed the girl I left be - hind me.
shared the glo - ry of that fight, sweet girl I left be - hind me.
wor - thy of his sire each son, sweet girl I left be - hind me.

Additional Lyrics

4. The hope of final victory
   Within my bosom burning
   Is mingled with sweet thoughts of thee,
   And of my fond returning.
   But should I ne'er return again,
   Still worth thy love thou'lt find me;
   Dishonor's breath shall never stain
   The name I leave behind me.

5. The dames of France are fond and free,
   And Flemish lips are willing,
   And soft the maids of Italy,
   While Spanish eyes are thrilling.
   Still though I bask beneath their smile,
   Their charms quite fail to bind me,
   And my heart falls back to Erin's Isle
   To the girl I left behind me.

GO DOWN, MOSES

Traditional American Spiritual

GRANDFATHER'S CLOCK

By HENRY CLAY WORK

Moderately

My grand - fa - ther's clock was too large for the shelf so it
watch - ing its pen - du - lum swing to and fro man - y
grand - fa - ther said that of those he could hire, not a
rang an a - larm in the dead of the night, an a -

stood nine - ty years on the floor. It was
hours had he spent while a boy. And in
ser - vant so faith - ful he found. For it
larm that for years had been dumb. And we

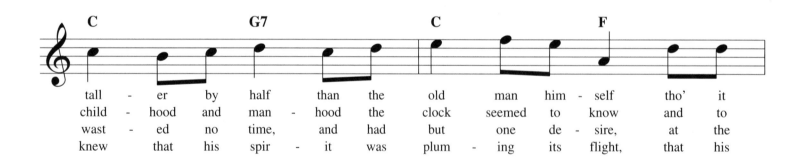

tall - er by half than the old man him - self tho' it
child - hood and man - hood the old clock seemed to know and to
wast - ed no time, and had but one de - sire, at the
knew that his spir - it was plum - ing its flight, that his

weighed not a pen - ny - weight more. It was
share both his grief and his joy. For it
close of each week to be wound. And it
hour of de - par - ture had come. Still the

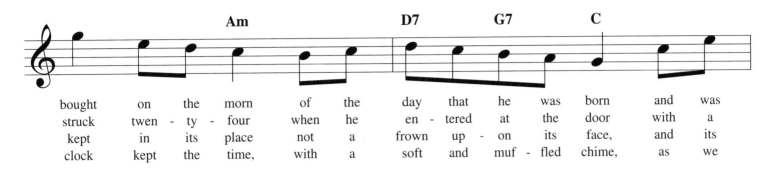

bought on the morn of the day that he was born and was
struck twen - ty - four when he en - tered at the door with a
kept in its place not a frown up - on its face, and its
clock kept the time, with a soft and muf - fled chime, as we

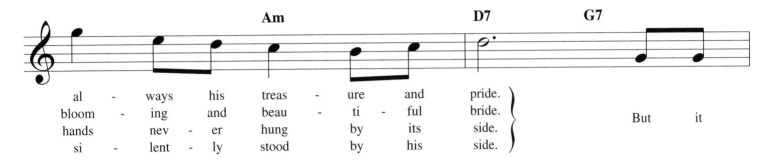

al - ways his treas - ure and pride.
bloom - ing and beau - ti - ful bride.
hands nev - er hung by its side.
si - lent - ly stood by his side.

But it

stopped short, nev - er to go a - gain, when the old man ___

died. Nine - ty years with - out slum - ber - ing, tick, tock, tick, tock, his

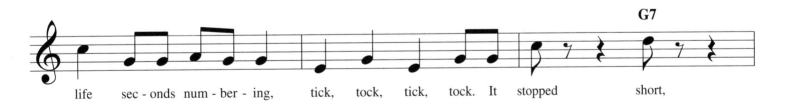

life sec - onds num - ber - ing, tick, tock, tick, tock. It stopped short,

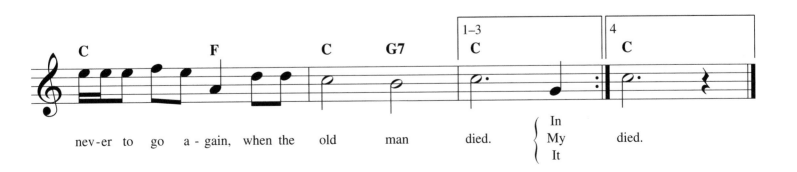

nev - er to go a - gain, when the old man died.

In
My died.
It

GREEN GROW THE LILACS

American Folksong

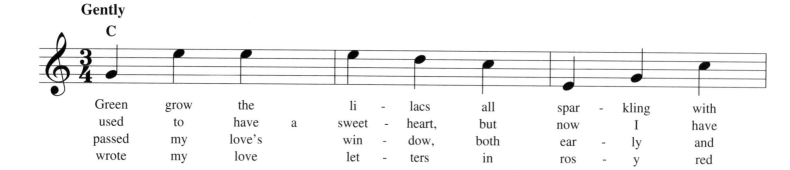

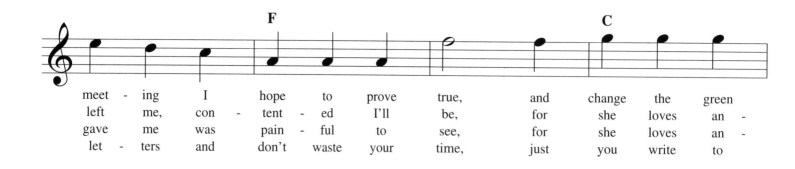

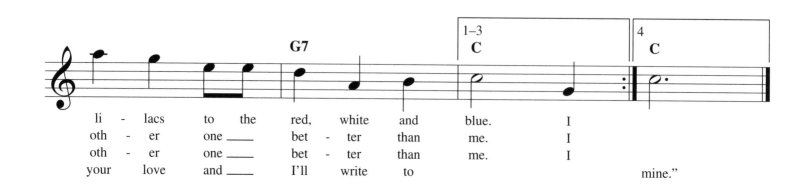

GREENSLEEVES

16th Century Traditional English

A - las,   my   love, _____ you   do   me   wrong _____ to
I   have   loved _____ you,   oh,   so   long, _____ de -

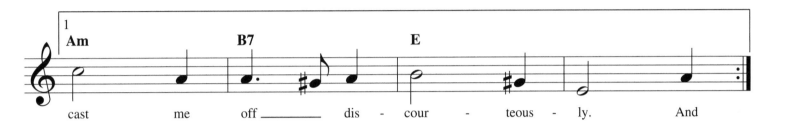

cast   me   off _____ dis - cour - teous - ly.   And

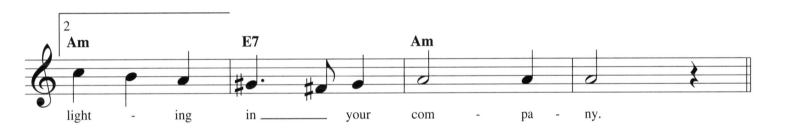

light - ing   in _____ your   com - pa - ny.

Green - sleeves _____ was   all   my   joy. _____
Green - sleeves   was   my   heart   of   gold, _____ and

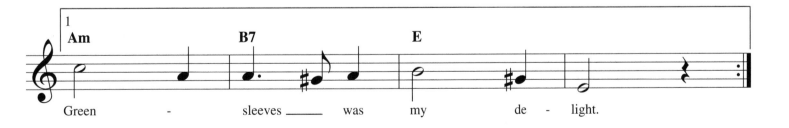

Green - sleeves _____ was   my   de - light.

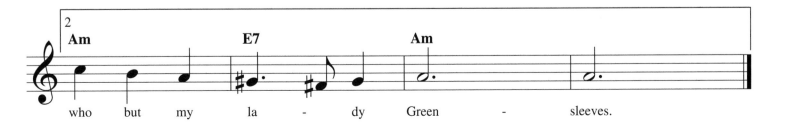

who   but   my   la - dy   Green - sleeves.

HATIKVAH
(With Hope)

Traditional Hebrew Melody
Lyrics by N.H. IMBER

Stately

Kol ___ od ba - lé - vav p' - ni - ma

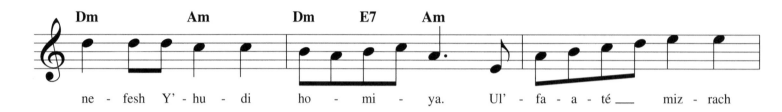

ne - fesh Y' - hu - di ho - mi - ya. Ul' - fa - a - té ___ miz - rach

ka - di - ma a - yin l' - tsi - yon tso - fi - ya.

Od lo av - da tik - va - té - nu, ha - tik - va bat

sh'not al - pa - yim. Li - yot am chof - shi b' - ar - tsé - nu

e - rets Tsi - yon Y' - ru - sha - la - yim. Li - yot am chof - shi

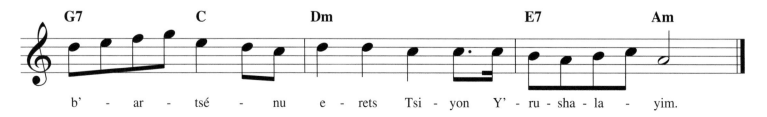

b' - ar - tsé - nu e - rets Tsi - yon Y' - ru - sha - la - yim.

HE'S GOT THE WHOLE WORLD IN HIS HANDS

Traditional Spiritual

HAVA NAGILA
(Let's Be Happy)

Lyrics by MOSHE NATHANSON
Music by ABRAHAM Z. IDELSOHN

Rhythmically

Ha - va _____ na - gi - la Ha - va _____ na - gi - la

Ha - va _____ na - gi - la v' - nis m' - cha,

Ha - va _____ na - gi - la Ha - va _____ na - gi - la

Ha - va _____ na - gi - la v' - nis m' - cha.

Ha - va n' - ra - n' na, Ha - va n' - ra - n' na,

Ha - va n' - ra - n' na, v' - nis m' - cha.

Ha - va n' - ra - n' na, Ha - va n' - ra - n' na,

Ha - va n' - ra - n' na, v' - nis m' - cha.

U - ru, U - ru a - chim,

U - ru a - chim B' - lev sa - mey - ach, U - ru a - chim B' -

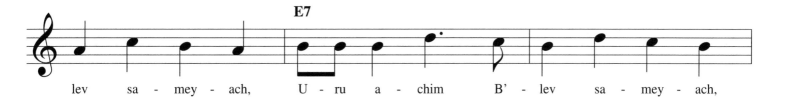

lev sa - mey - ach, U - ru a - chim B' - lev sa - mey - ach,

U - ru a - chim B' - lev sa - mey - ach. U - ru a - chim,

U - ru a - chim B' lev sa - mey - ach.

HOME ON THE RANGE

Lyrics by DR. BREWSTER HIGLEY
Music by DAN KELLY

Slowly

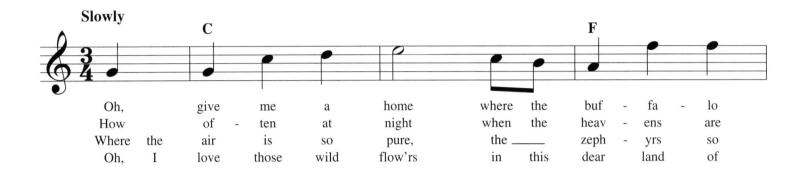

Oh, give me a home where the buf - fa - lo
How of - ten at night when the heav - ens are
Where the air is so pure, the _____ zeph - yrs so
Oh, I love those wild flow'rs in this dear land of

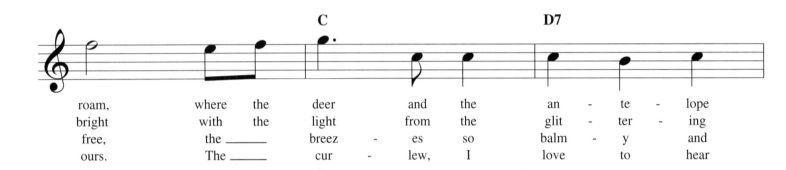

roam, where the deer and the an - te - lope
bright with the light from the glit - ter - ing
free, the _____ breez - es so balm - y and
ours. The _____ cur - lew, I love to hear

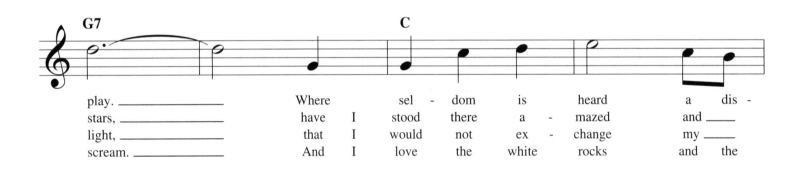

play. _____ Where sel - dom is heard a dis -
stars, _____ have I stood there a - mazed and _____
light, _____ that I would not ex - change my _____
scream. _____ And I love the white rocks and the

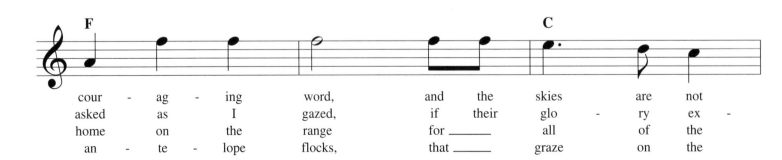

cour - ag - ing word, and the skies are not
asked as I gazed, if their glo - ry ex -
home on the range for _____ all of the
an - te - lope flocks, that _____ graze on the

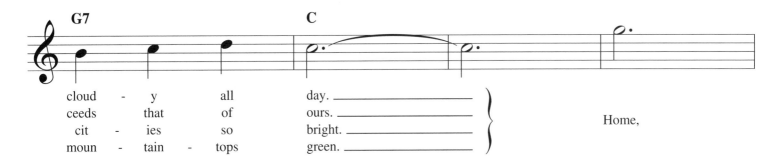

cloud - y all day. _____
ceeds that of ours. _____
cit - ies so bright. _____
moun - tain - tops green. _____

Home,

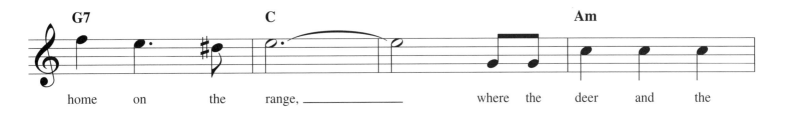

home on the range, _____ where the deer and the

an - te - lope play. _____ Where sel - dom is

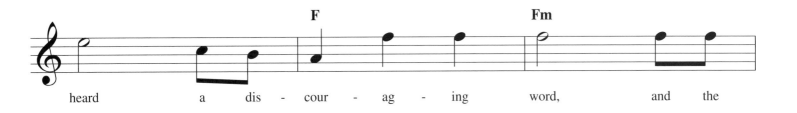

heard a dis - cour - ag - ing word, and the

skies are not cloud - y all day. _____

HOME SWEET HOME

Words by JOHN HOWARD PAYNE
Music by HENRY R. BISHOP

Gently

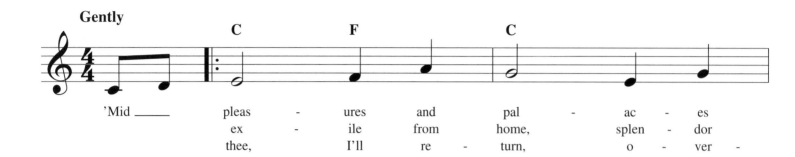

'Mid _____ pleas - ures and pal - ac - es
ex - ile from home, splen - dor
thee, I'll re - turn, o - ver -

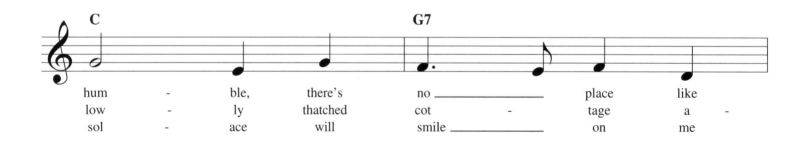

though _____ we may roam, be it ev - er so
daz - zles in vain, oh, _____ give me my
bur - dened with care, the _____ heart's dear - est

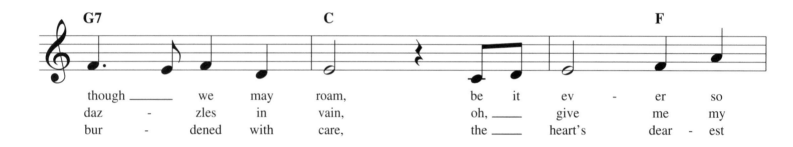

hum - ble, there's no _____ place like
low - ly thatched cot - tage a -
sol - ace will smile _____ on me

home. A charm _____ from the sky seems to
gain. The birds _____ sing - ing gai - ly, that
there. No more _____ from that cot - tage a -

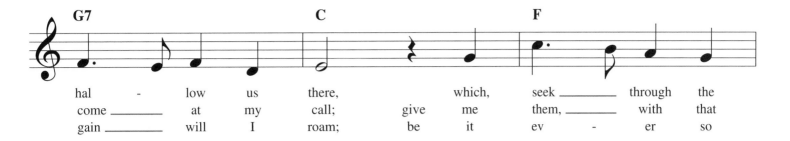

hal - low us there, which, seek _____ through the
come _____ at my call; give me them, _____ with that
gain _____ will I roam; be it ev - er so

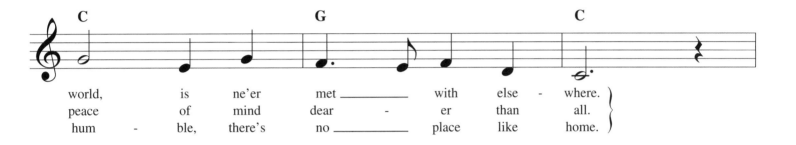

world, is ne'er met _____ with else - where.
peace of mind dear - er than all.
hum - ble, there's no _____ place like home.

Home! Home! Sweet home. _____ There's no _____ place like

home. Home! Home! Sweet home. _____ There's

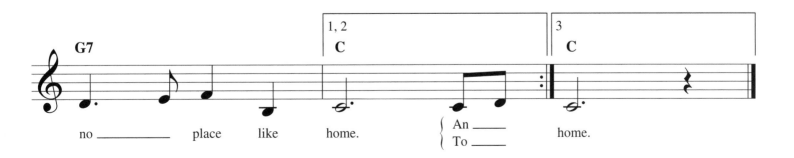

no _____ place like home. An _____ home.
To _____

HOUSE OF THE RISING SUN

Southern American Folksong

Moderately

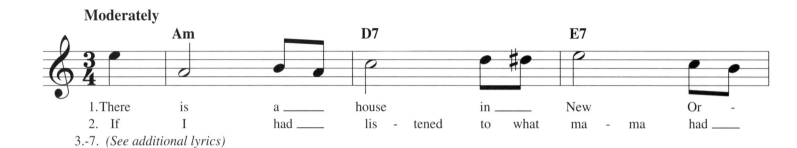

1. There is a _____ house in _____ New Or -
2. If I had ____ lis - tened to what ma - ma had ____

3.-7. *(See additional lyrics)*

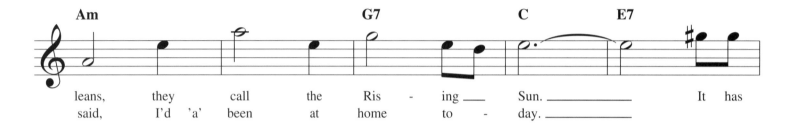

leans, they call the Ris - ing ____ Sun. _____ It has
said, I'd 'a' been at home to - day. _____

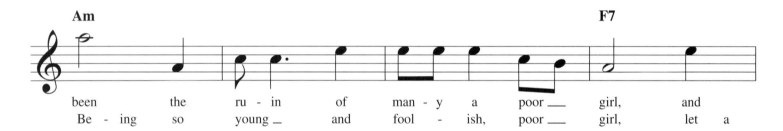

been the ru - in of man - y a poor ____ girl, and
Be - ing so young ____ and fool - ish, poor ____ girl, let a

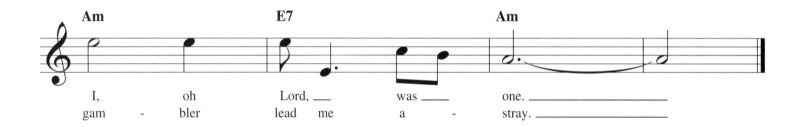

I, oh Lord, ____ was ____ one. _____
gam - bler lead me a - stray. _____

Additional Lyrics

3. My mother, she's a tailor,
   She sells those new blue jeans.
   My sweetheart, he's a drunkard, Lord,
   Drink down in New Orleans.

4. The only thing a drunkard needs
   Is a suitcase and a trunk.
   The only time he's satisfied
   Is when he's on a drunk.

5. Go tell my baby sister,
   Never do like I have done.
   To shun that house in New Orleans
   They call the Rising Sun.

6. One foot is on the platform,
   And the other is on the train.
   I'm going back to New Orleans
   To wear the ball and chain.

7. I'm going back to New Orleans,
   My race is almost run.
   Going back to end my life
   Beneath the Rising Sun.

I GAVE MY LOVE A CHERRY
(The Riddle Song)

Traditional

Moderately

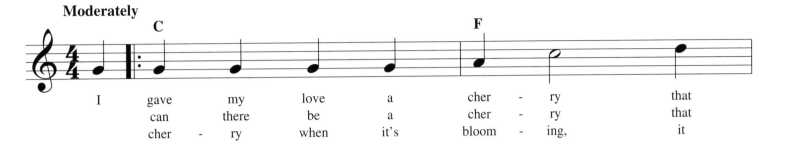

I gave my love a cher - ry that
can there be a cher - ry that
cher - ry when it's bloom - ing, it

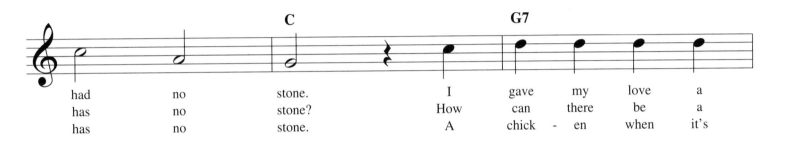

had no stone. I gave my love a
has no stone? How can there be a
has no stone. A chick - en when it's

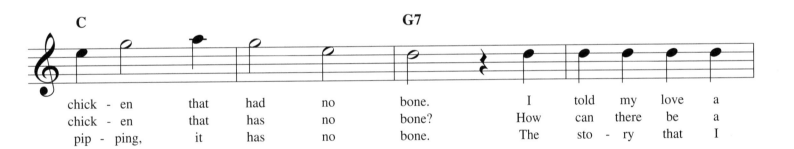

chick - en that had no bone. I told my love a
chick - en that has no bone? How can there be a
pip - ping, it has no bone. The sto - ry that I

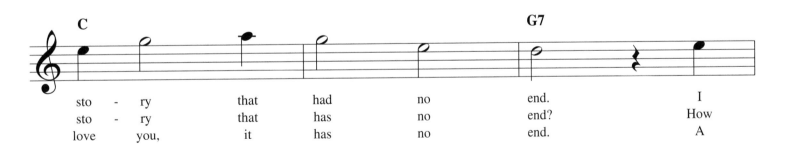

sto - ry that had no end. I
sto - ry that has no end? How
love you, it has no end. A

gave my love a ba - by with no cry - in'. How
can there be a ba - by with no cry - in'? A
ba - by, when it's sleep - ing, has no cry - in'.

I'VE BEEN WORKING ON THE RAILROAD

American Folksong

Brightly

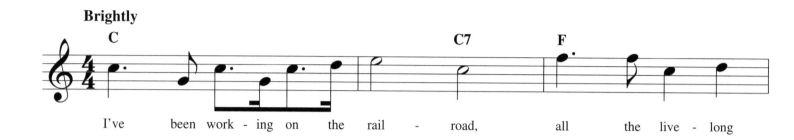

I've been work - ing on the rail - road, all the live - long

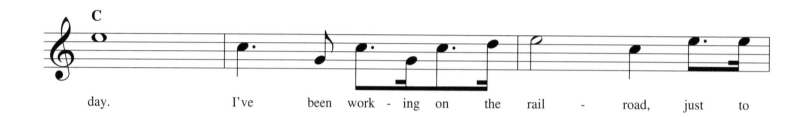

day. I've been work - ing on the rail - road, just to

pass the time a - way. Can't you hear the whis - tle

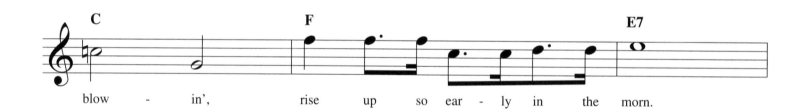

blow - in', rise up so ear - ly in the morn.

Can't you hear the cap - tain shout - in', "Di - nah, blow your horn!"

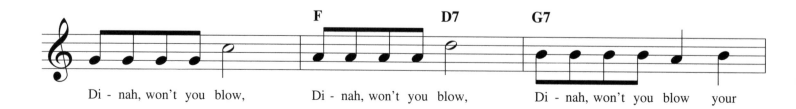

Di - nah, won't you blow, Di - nah, won't you blow, Di - nah, won't you blow your

horn? _____ Di - nah, won't you blow, Di - nah, won't you blow,

Di - nah, won't you blow your horn? Some-one's in the kitch - en with

Di - nah. Some-one's in the kitch - en I know. _____

Some-one's in the kitch - en with Di - nah, strum - min' on the old ban -

jo, and sing - in', "Fee, fi, fid - dle - ee - i - o,

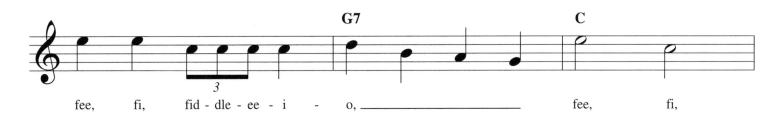

fee, fi, fid - dle - ee - i - o, _____ fee, fi,

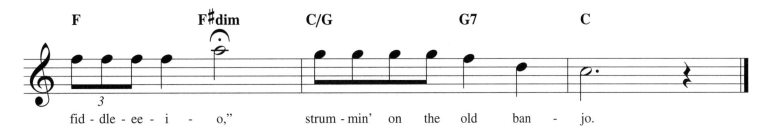

fid - dle - ee - i - o," strum - min' on the old ban - jo.

I'VE GOT PEACE LIKE A RIVER

Traditional

Moderately

I've got peace like a riv - er. I've got peace like a
I've got love like an o - cean. I've got peace love like an
I've got joy like a foun - tain. I've got joy like a

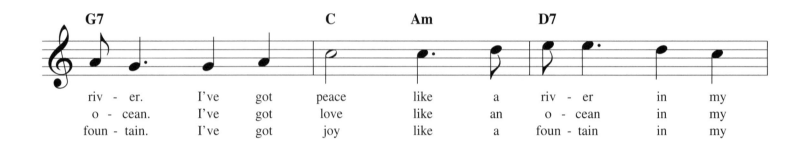

riv - er. I've got peace like a riv - er in my
o - cean. I've got love like an o - cean in my
foun - tain. I've got joy like a foun - tain in my

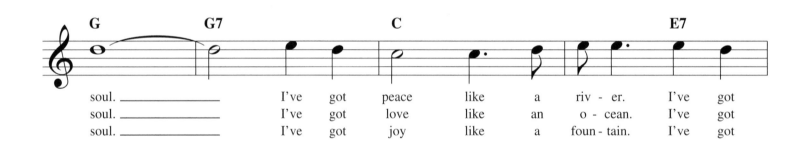

soul. _____ I've got peace like a riv - er. I've got
soul. _____ I've got love like an o - cean. I've got
soul. _____ I've got joy like a foun - tain. I've got

peace like a riv - er. I've got peace like a
love like an o - cean. I've got love like an
joy like a foun - tain. I've got joy like a

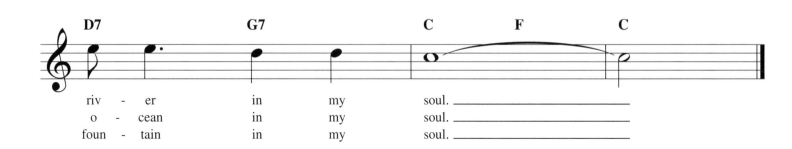

riv - er in my soul. _____
o - cean in my soul. _____
foun - tain in my soul. _____

IF YOU'RE HAPPY AND YOU KNOW IT

Words and Music by
L. SMITH

If you're hap - py and you know it, { clap your hands. / stamp your foot. / nod your head. / turn a - round. / touch your nose. }   If you're

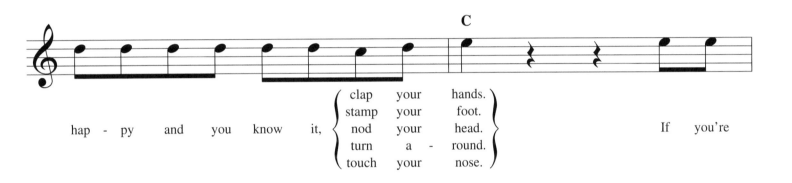

hap - py and you know it, { clap your hands. / stamp your foot. / nod your head. / turn a - round. / touch your nose. }   If you're

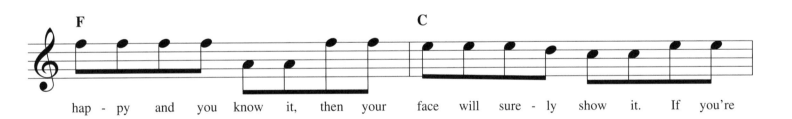

hap - py and you know it, then your face will sure - ly show it. If you're

hap - py and you know it, { clap your hands. / stamp your foot. / nod your head. / turn a - round. / touch your nose. }

JEANIE WITH THE LIGHT BROWN HAIR

Words and Music by
STEPHEN C. FOSTER

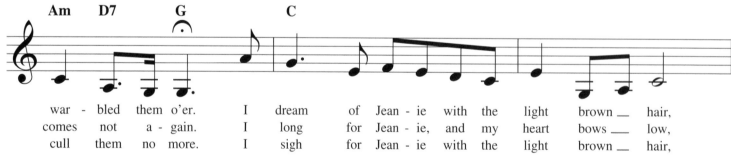

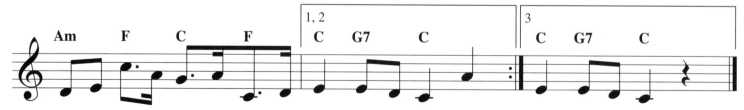

JENNY JENKINS

18th Century American Folksong

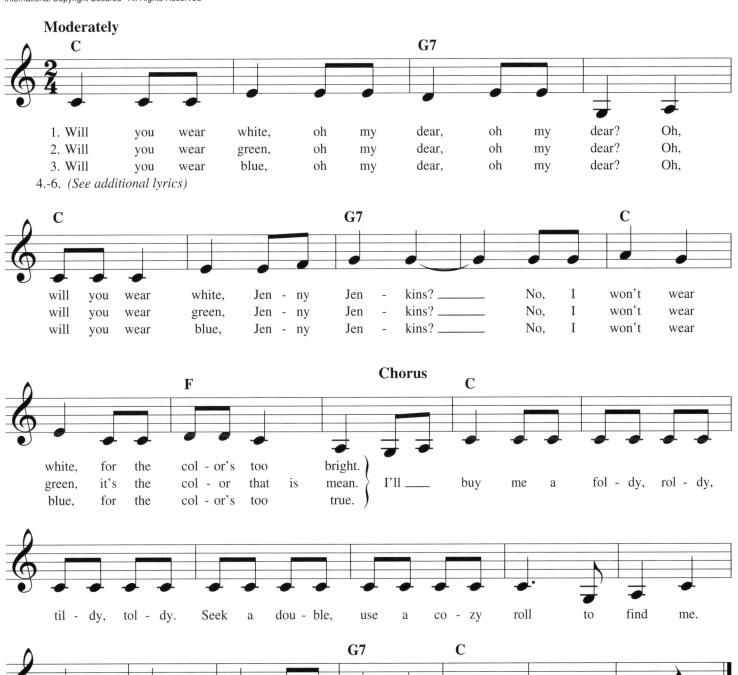

1. Will you wear white, oh my dear, oh my dear? Oh,
2. Will you wear green, oh my dear, oh my dear? Oh,
3. Will you wear blue, oh my dear, oh my dear? Oh,

4.-6. *(See additional lyrics)*

will you wear white, Jen - ny Jen - kins? _____ No, I won't wear
will you wear green, Jen - ny Jen - kins? _____ No, I won't wear
will you wear blue, Jen - ny Jen - kins? _____ No, I won't wear

Chorus

white, for the col - or's too bright.
green, it's the col - or that is mean. } I'll ___ buy me a fol - dy, rol - dy,
blue, for the col - or's too true.

til - dy, tol - dy. Seek a dou - ble, use a co - zy roll to find me.

Roll, _____ Jen - ny Jen - kins, roll. _____

Additional Lyrics

4. Will you wear yellow, oh my dear, oh my dear?
   Oh, will you wear yellow, Jenny Jenkins?
   No, I won't wear yellow, for I'd never get a fellow.
   Chorus

5. Will you wear brown, oh my dear, oh my dear?
   Oh, will you wear brown, Jenny Jenkins?
   No, I won't wear brown, for I'd never get around.
   Chorus

6. Will you wear beige, oh my dear, oh my dear?
   Oh, will you wear beige, Jenny Jenkins?
   No, I won't wear beige, for it shows my age.
   Chorus

JOHN HENRY

West Virginia Folksong

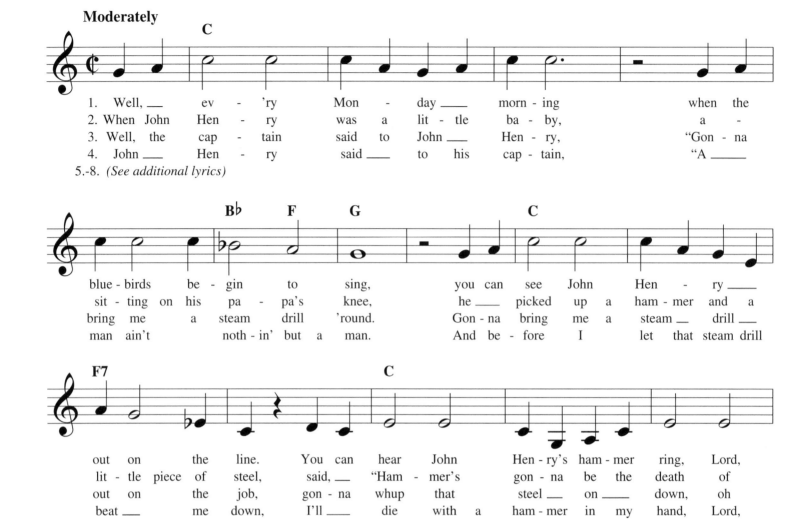

Additional Lyrics

5. John Henry said to his shaker,
   He said, "Shaker, why don't you pray?
   'Cause if I miss this little piece of steel,
   Tomorrow be your buryin' day, yes sir,
   Tomorrow be your buryin' day."

6. John Henry was driving on the mountain,
   And his hammer was flashing fire.
   And the last words I heard that poor boy say:
   "Gimme a cool drink of water 'fore I die, Lord,
   Lord, gimme a cool drink of water 'fore I die."

7. John Henry, he drove fifteen feet,
   The steam drill only made nine.
   But he hammered so hard that he broke his poor heart,
   And he laid down his hammer and he died,
   And he laid down his hammer and he died.

8. They took John Henry to the graveyard
   And they buried him in the sand.
   And every locomotive comes a-roaring by says,
   "There lies a steel-driving man,
   There lies a steel-driving man."

LA CUCARACHA

Mexican Revolutionary Folksong

LITTLE BROWN JUG

Words and Music by
JOSEPH E. WINNER

Gaily

My wife and I lived all a - lone in a
you who makes my all friends my foes; 'tis _____

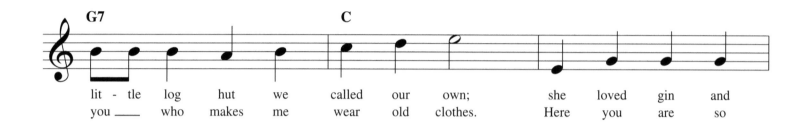

lit - tle log hut we called our own; she loved gin and
you _____ who makes me wear old clothes. Here you are so

I loved rum, I tell you what, we'd lots of fun!
near my nose, so tip her up and down she goes!

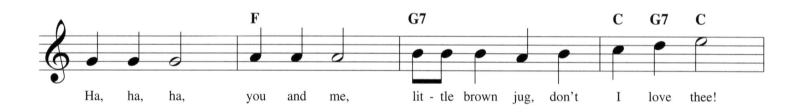

Ha, ha, ha, you and me, lit - tle brown jug, don't I love thee!

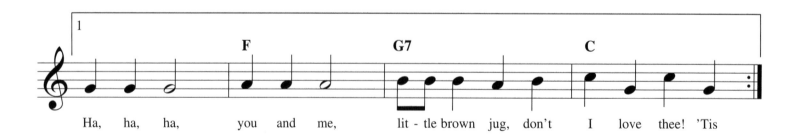

1.
Ha, ha, ha, you and me, lit - tle brown jug, don't I love thee! 'Tis

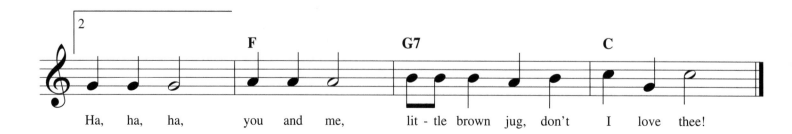

2.
Ha, ha, ha, you and me, lit - tle brown jug, don't I love thee!

LOCH LOMOND

Scottish Folksong

THE MAN ON THE FLYING TRAPEZE

Words by GEORGE LEYBOURNE
Music by ALFRED LEE

Rhythmically

1. Oh, once I was hap - py, but now I'm for - lorn, Just

2.-5. *(See additional lyrics)*

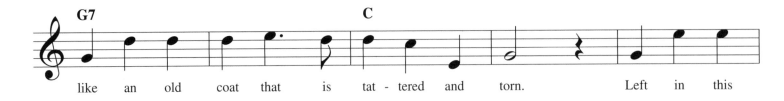

like an old coat that is tat - tered and torn. Left in this

wide world to fret and to mourn, Be - trayed by a maid in her

teens. _____ Now, this girl that I loved she was hand - some, _____

_____ And I tried all I knew her to please. _____ But I

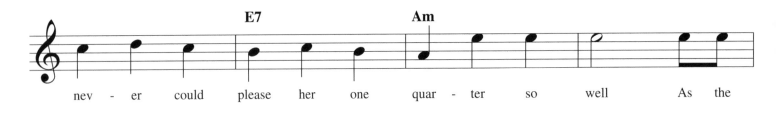

nev - er could please her one quar - ter so well As the

Chorus

man on the fly - ing tra - peze. Oh! He'd float through the

air with the great - est of ease, This dar - ing young man on the

fly - ing tra - peze. His move - ments are grace - ful, all girls he does

please, And my love he has pur - loined a - way. _____

Additional Lyrics

2. Now the young man by name was Señor Boni Slang,
   Tall, big and handsome, as well made as Chang.
   Where'er he appeared, how the hall loudly rang,
   With ovations from all people there.
   He'd smile from the bar on the people below
   And one night he smiled on my love,
   She winked back at him, and she shouted "Bravo!"
   As he hung by his nose from above.
   Chorus

3. Her father and mother were both on my side
   And tried very hard to make her my bride.
   Her father, he signed, and her mother, she cried
   To see her throw herself away.
   'Twas all no avail, she went there ev'ry night
   And threw her bouquets on the stage,
   Which caused him to meet her—how he ran me down,
   To tell it would take a whole page.
   Chorus

4. One night I as usual went to her dear home,
   And found there her mother and father alone.
   I asked for my love, and soon 'twas made known,
   To my horror, that she's run away.
   She packed up her boxes and eloped in the night,
   With him with the greatest of ease.
   From two stories high he had lowered her down
   To the ground on his flying trapeze.
   Chorus

5. Some months after that I went into a hall;
   To my surprise I found there on the wall
   A bill in red letters which did my heart gall,
   That she was appearing with him.
   He'd taught her gymnastics, and dressed her in tights
   To help him live at ease.
   He'd made her assume a masculine name,
   And now she goes on the trapeze.

Final Chorus:
She floats through the air with the greatest of ease;
You'd think her a man on the flying trapeze.
She does all the work while he takes his ease,
And that's what's become of my love.

MATILDA

Traditional Folksong

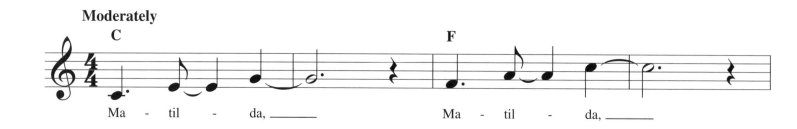

Ma - til - da, _____ Ma - til - da, _____

Ma - til - da, she take me mon - ey and run Ven - e - zue - la! ___

That wom - an made a wreck of me,
I save up, gon - na make her my wife, but she
We were sleep - ing in me bed,
What to do and where to go?

what she done to me you ought to see. ___
want - a live an - oth - er kind of life. ___
when she found the mon - ey me had hid. ___
Nev - er trust a wom - an with your dough. __

Ma - til - da, she

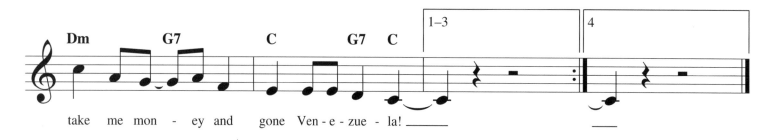

take me mon - ey and gone Ven - e - zue - la! ___

MEXICAN HAT DANCE
(Jarabe Topatio)

By F.A. PARTICHELA

MRS. MURPHY'S CHOWDER

Irish Folksong

Won't you bring back, won't you bring back
Won't you bring back, won't you bring back
Won't you bring back, won't you bring back

Mis - sus Mur - phy's chow - der? It was tune - ful, ev - 'ry
Mis - sus Mur - phy's chow - der? From each help - ing, you'll be
Mis - sus Mur - phy's chow - der? You can pack it, you can

spoon - ful made you yo - del loud - er.
yelp - ing for a head - ache pow - der. And
stack it all a - round the lard - er. The

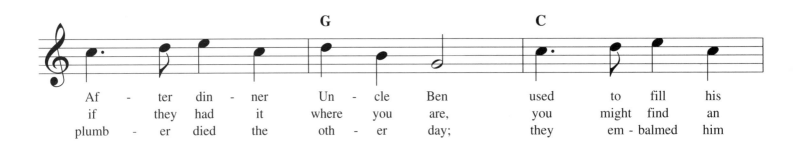

Af - ter din - ner Un - cle Ben used to fill his
if they had it where you are, you might find an
plumb - er died the oth - er day; they em - balmed him

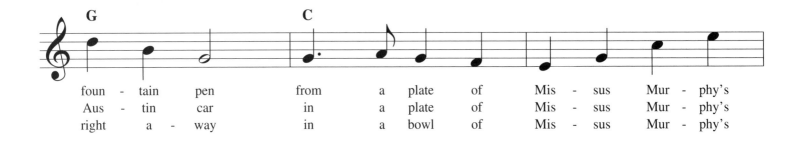

foun - tain pen from a plate of Mis - sus Mur - phy's
Aus - tin car in a plate of Mis - sus Mur - phy's
right a - way in a bowl of Mis - sus Mur - phy's

chow - der.
chow - der.
chow - der.

It had ice cream, cold cream,

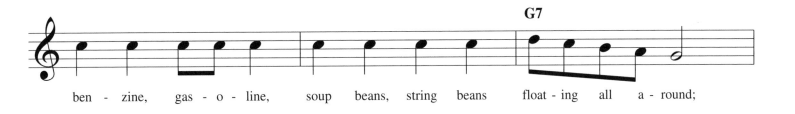

ben - zine, gas - o - line, soup beans, string beans float - ing all a - round;

sponge cake, beef steak, mis - take, stom - ach ache, cream puffs, ear - muffs,

man - y to be found. Silk hats, door - mats, bed slats, Dem - o - crats,

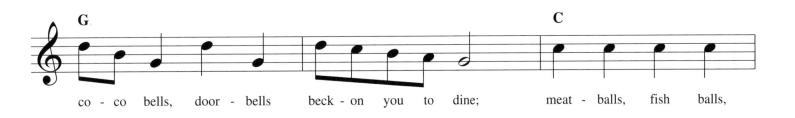

co - co bells, door - bells beck - on you to dine; meat - balls, fish balls,

moth balls, can - non balls, come on in, the chow - der's fine.

MY BONNIE LIES OVER THE OCEAN

Traditional

Moderately

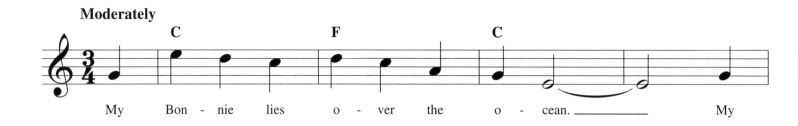

My Bon - nie lies o - ver the o - cean. _____ My

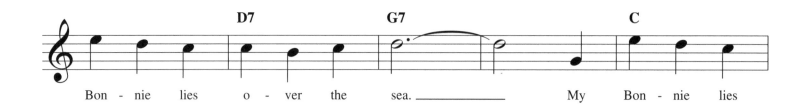

Bon - nie lies o - ver the sea. _____ My Bon - nie lies

o - ver the o - cean. _____ Oh, bring back my Bon - nie to

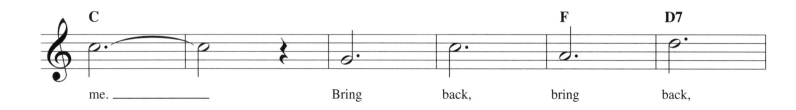

me. _____ Bring back, bring back,

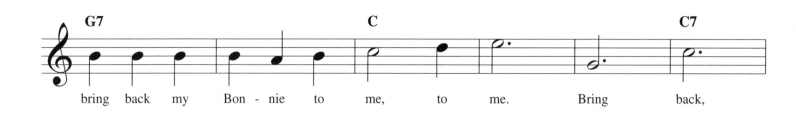

bring back my Bon - nie to me, to me. Bring back,

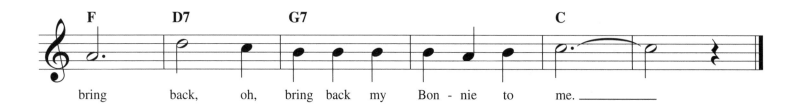

bring back, oh, bring back my Bon - nie to me. _____

MY WILD IRISH ROSE

Words and Music by
CHAUNCEY OLCOTT

Slowly, with much expression

MY OLD KENTUCKY HOME

Words and Music by
STEPHEN C. FOSTER

Slowly

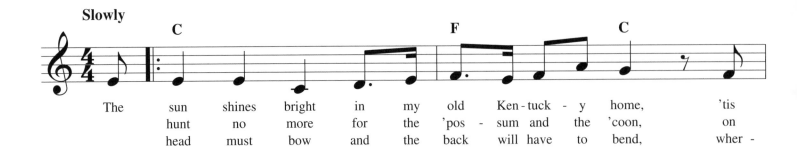

The   sun   shines   bright   in   my   old   Ken - tuck - y   home,   'tis
hunt   no   more   for   the   'pos - sum   and   the   'coon,   on
head   must   bow   and   the   back   will   have   to   bend,   wher -

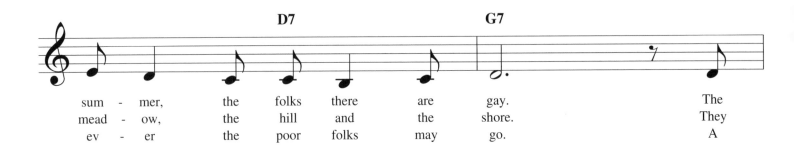

sum - mer,   the   folks   there   are   gay.   The
mead - ow,   the   hill   and   the   shore.   They
ev - er   the   poor   folks   may   go.   A

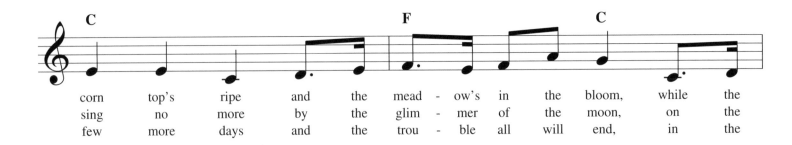

corn   top's   ripe   and   the   mead - ow's   in   the   bloom,   while   the
sing   no   more   by   the   glim - mer   of   the   moon,   on   the
few   more   days   and   the   trou - ble   all   will   end,   in   the

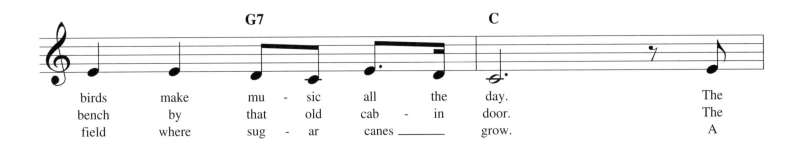

birds   make   mu - sic   all   the   day.   The
bench   by   that   old   cab - in   door.   The
field   where   sug - ar   canes _____ grow.   A

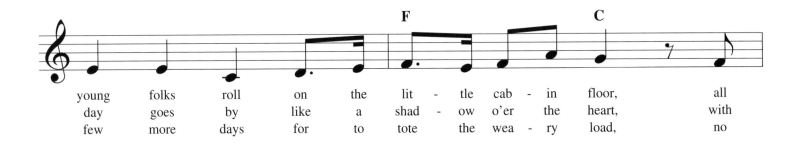

young   folks   roll   on   the   lit - tle   cab - in   floor,   all
day   goes   by   like   a   shad - ow   o'er   the   heart,   with
few   more   days   for   to   tote   the   wea - ry   load,   no

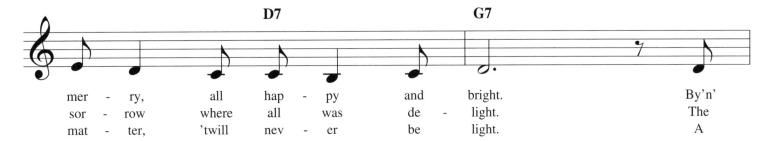

D7   **G7**

mer - ry,   all   hap - py   and   bright.   By'n'
sor - row   where   all   was   de - light.   The
mat - ter,   'twill   nev - er   be   light.   A

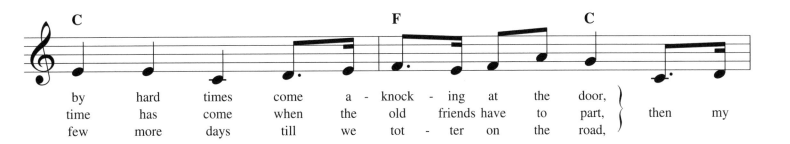

C   **F**   **C**

by   hard   times   come   a - knock - ing   at   the   door,   then   my
time   hard   has   come   when   the   old   friends have   to   part,   then   my
few   more   days   till   we   tot - ter   on   the   road,

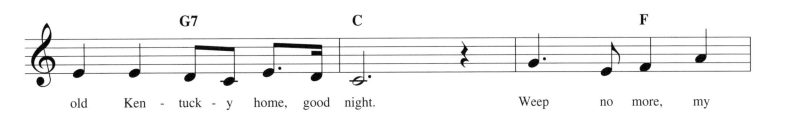

G7   **C**   **F**

old   Ken - tuck - y   home,   good   night.   Weep   no   more,   my

C   **F**   **C**

la - dy,   oh,   weep   no   more   to - day.   We   will

                                             F   **C**

sing   one   song   for   the   old   Ken - tuck - y   home,   for   the

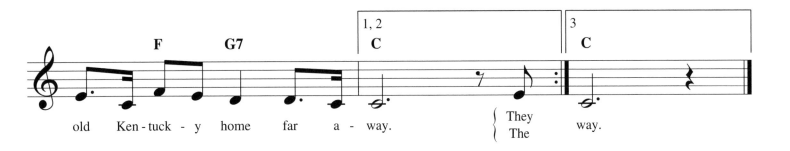

                        F   **G7**   **1, 2**   **3**
                                                                C   **C**

old   Ken - tuck - y   home   far   a - way.   { They   way.
                                                         { The

NOBODY KNOWS THE TROUBLE I'VE SEEN

African-American Spiritual

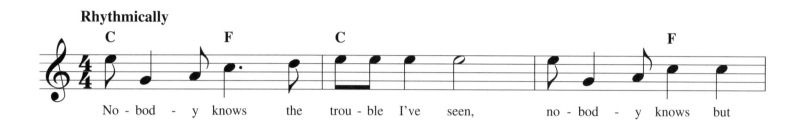

No - bod - y knows the trou - ble I've seen, no - bod - y knows but

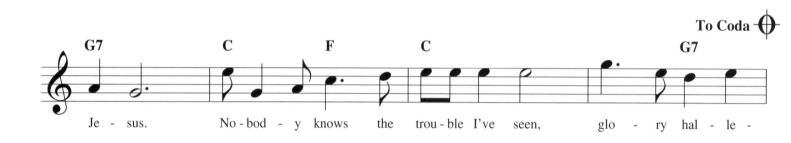

Je - sus. No - bod - y knows the trou - ble I've seen, glo - ry hal - le -

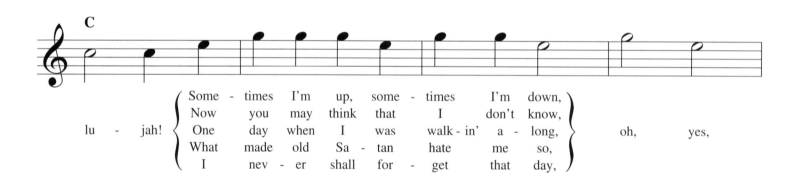

lu - jah!

| Some - times I'm up, some - times I'm down, |
| Now you may think that I don't know, |
| One day when I was walk - in' a - long, |
| What made old Sa - tan hate me so, |
| I nev - er shall for - get that day, |

oh, yes,

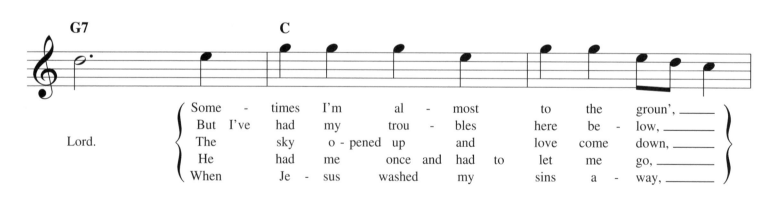

Lord.

| Some - times I'm al - most to the groun', _____ |
| But I've had my trou - bles here be - low, _____ |
| The sky o - pened up and love come down, _____ |
| He had me once and had to let me go, _____ |
| When Je - sus washed my sins a - way, _____ |

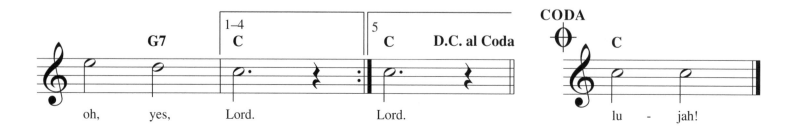

oh, yes, Lord.   Lord.   lu - jah!

'O SOLE MIO

Words by GIOVANNI CAPURRO
Music by EDUARDO DI CAPUA

OH! SUSANNA

Words and Music by
STEPHEN C. FOSTER

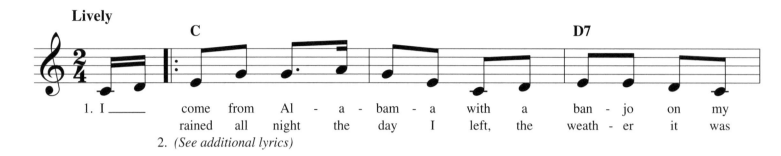

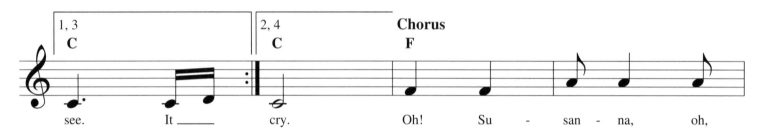

Additional Lyrics

2. I had a dream the other night
   When everything was still.
   I thought I saw Susanna
   A-coming down the hill.
   The buckwheat cake was in her mouth,
   The tear was in her eye,
   Say I, "I'm coming from the South.
   Susanna, don't you cry."
   Chorus

OLD BLACK JOE

Words and Music by
STEPHEN C. FOSTER

Slowly

Gone   are   the   days   when my   heart   was   young   and   gay,
Why   do   I   weep   when my   heart   should   feel   no   pain,
Where   are   the   hearts   once   so   hap - py   and   so   free,   the

gone   are   my   friends   from   the   cot - ton   fields   a - way,
why   do   I   sigh   that   my   friends   come   not   a - gain,
chil - dren,   so   dear,   that   I   held   up - on   my   knee?

gone   from   the   earth   to   a   bet - ter   land   I   know.
griev - ing   for   forms   now   de - part - ed   long   a - go?   I
Gone   to   the   shore   where   my   soul   has   longed   to   go.

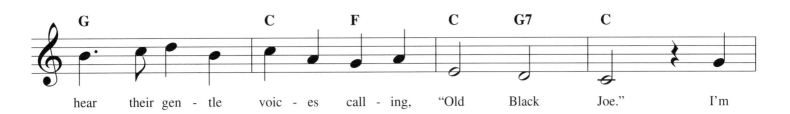

hear   their   gen - tle   voic - es   call - ing,   "Old   Black   Joe."   I'm

com - ing,   I'm   com - ing,   for   my   head   is   bend - ing   low;   I

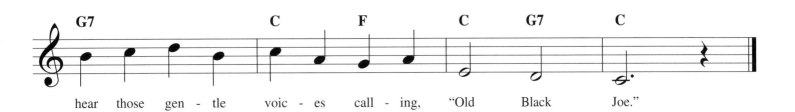

hear   those   gen - tle   voic - es   call - ing,   "Old   Black   Joe."

OLD FOLKS AT HOME
(Swanee River)

Words and Music by
STEPHEN C. FOSTER

Moderately

Way down up - on the Swan - ee Riv - er,
All 'round the lit - tle farm I wan - der'd,
One lit - tle hut a - mong the bush - es,

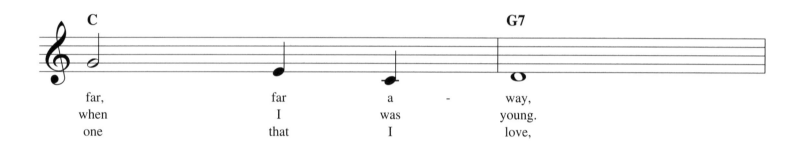

far, far a - way,
when I was young.
one that I love,

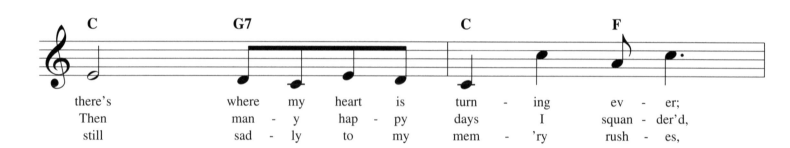

there's where my heart is turn - ing ev - er;
Then man - y hap - py days I squan - der'd,
still sad - ly to my mem - 'ry rush - es,

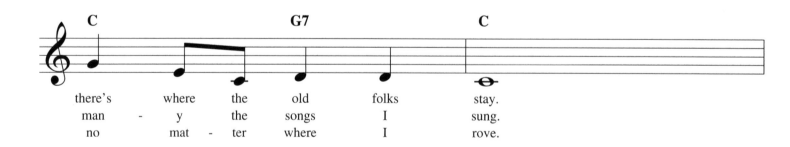

there's where the old folks stay.
man - y the songs I sung.
no mat - ter where I rove.

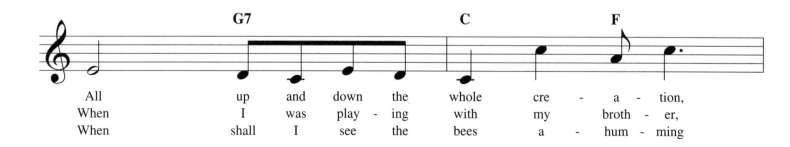

All up and down the whole cre - a - tion,
When I was play - ing with my broth - er,
When shall I see the bees a - hum - ming

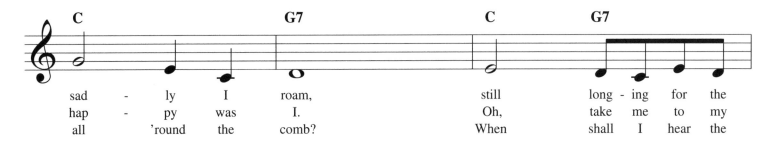

sad - ly I roam, still long - ing for the
hap - py was I. Oh, take me to my
all 'round the comb? When shall I hear the

old plan - ta - tion and for the old folks at home.
kind old moth - er, there let me live and ___ die.
ban - jo strum - ming down in my good old ___ home?

All the world is sad and drear - y ev - 'ry - where I

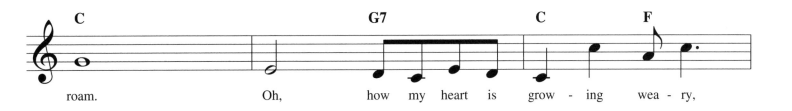

roam. Oh, how my heart is grow - ing wea - ry,

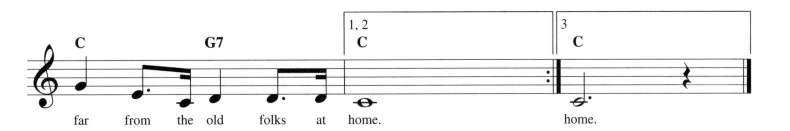

far from the old folks at home. home.

THE OLD GRAY MARE

Words and Music by
J. WARNER

Moderately

Oh, the old gray mare, she ain't what she used to be,

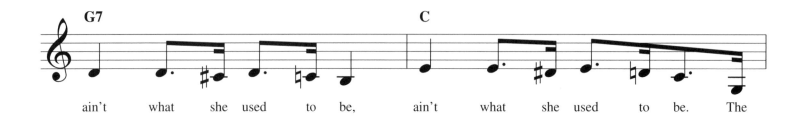

ain't what she used to be, ain't what she used to be. The

old gray mare, she ain't what she used to be man - y long years a -

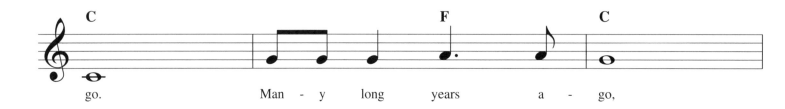

go. Man - y long years a - go,

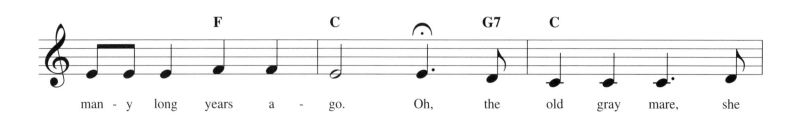

man - y long years a - go. Oh, the old gray mare, she

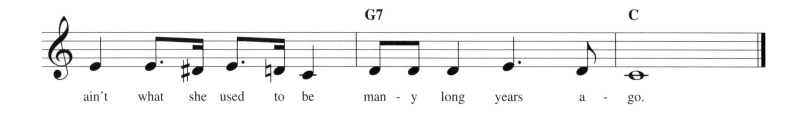

ain't what she used to be man - y long years a - go.

POLLY WOLLY DOODLE

Traditional American Minstrel Song

Steadily

1. Oh, I went down South for to see my Sal,
2. Oh, my Sal she is a ___ maid-en fair,
3. Oh, a grass-hop-per sit-tin' on a rail-road track,
4.-6. *(See additional lyrics)*

sing-ing pol-ly-wol-ly-doo-dle all the

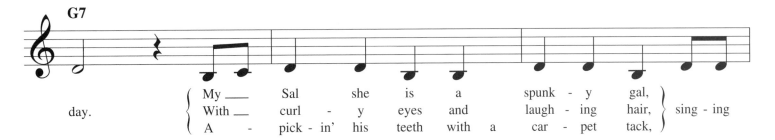

day.

My ___ Sal she is a spunk-y gal,
With ___ curl-y eyes and laugh-ing hair,
A-pick-in' his teeth with a car-pet tack,

sing-ing

Chorus

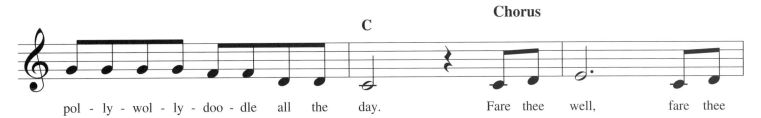

pol-ly-wol-ly-doo-dle all the day. Fare thee well, fare thee

well, fare thee well, my fair-y fay. For I'm goin' to Lou'-si-an-a for to

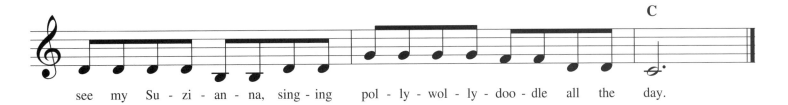

see my Su-zi-an-na, sing-ing pol-ly-wol-ly-doo-dle all the day.

Additional Lyrics

4. Oh, I went to bed, but it wasn't no use,
   Singing polly-wolly-doodle all the day.
   My feet stuck out like a chicken roost,
   Singing polly-wolly-doodle all the day.
   Chorus

5. Behind the barn, down on my knees,
   Singing polly-wolly-doodle all the day,
   I thought I heard a chicken sneeze,
   Singing polly-wolly-doodle all the day.
   Chorus

6. He sneezed so hard with the whooping cough,
   Singing polly-wolly-doodle all the day.
   He sneezed his head and tail right off,
   Singing polly-wolly-doodle all the day.
   Chorus

OVER THE WAVES

By JUVENTINO ROSAS

POP GOES THE WEASEL

Traditional

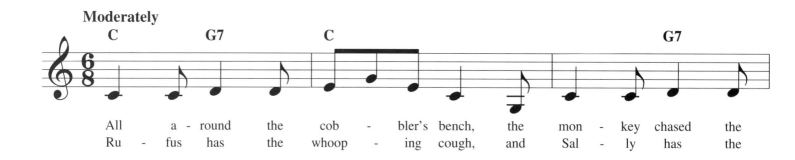

All a - round the cob - bler's bench, the mon - key chased the
Ru - fus has the whoop - ing cough, and Sal - ly has the

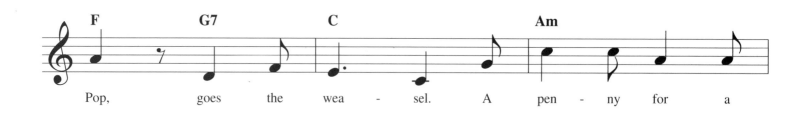

wea - sel. The mon - key thought 'twas all _____ in fun.
mea - sles. And that's the way the doc - tor goes.

Pop, goes the wea - sel. A pen - ny for a

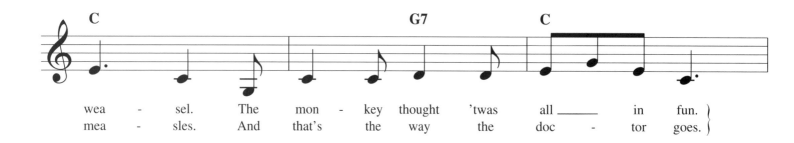

spool ___ of thread, a pen - ny for ___ a nee - dle.

That's the way the mon - key goes. Pop, goes the wea - sel.

THE RAMBLING SAILOR

English Sea Chantey

Moderately

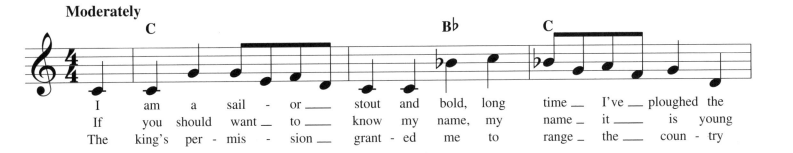

I   am   a   sail - or ___ stout and bold, long   time ___ I've ___ ploughed the
If   you should want ___ to ___ know   my   name, my   name ___ it ___ is young
The   king's per - mis - sion ___ grant - ed me   to   range ___ the ___ coun - try

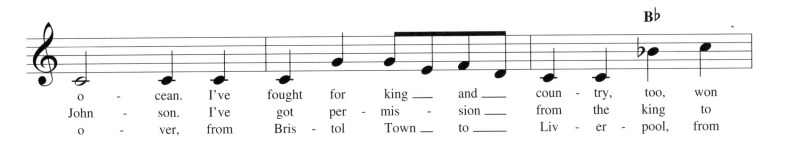

o - cean. I've fought for king ___ and ___ coun - try, too, won
John - son. I've got per - mis - sion ___ from the king to
o - ver, from Bris - tol Town ___ to ___ Liv - er - pool, from

hon - or ___ and pro - mo - tion. I   said: My broth - er sail - or, I
court ___ young ___ girls and hand - some. I   said: ___ My ___ dear, what ___
Ply - mouth ___ Sound to Do - ver. And   in ___ what - ev - er ___

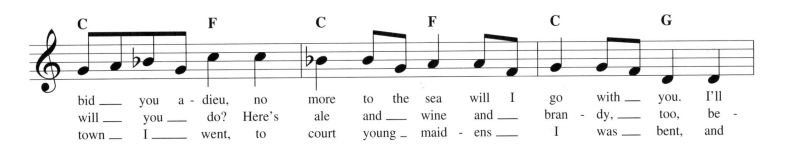

bid ___ you a - dieu, no   more to the sea will I   go with ___ you. I'll
will ___ you ___ do? Here's ale and ___ wine and ___ bran - dy, ___ too, be -
town ___ I ___ went, to court young ___ maid - ens ___ I   was ___ bent, and

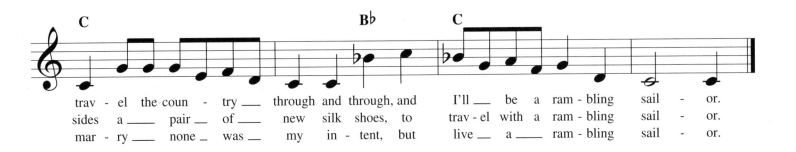

trav - el the coun - try ___ through and through, and   I'll ___ be a ram - bling sail - or.
sides a ___ pair ___ of ___ new silk shoes, to   trav - el with a ram - bling sail - or.
mar - ry ___ none ___ was ___ my in - tent, but   live ___ a ___ ram - bling sail - or.

THE RED RIVER VALLEY

Traditional American Cowboy Song

Come and sit by my side if you love me. ____
Won't you think of this val - ley you're leav - ing, ____
From this val - ley they say you are go - ing. ____
I have prom - ised you, dar - ling, that nev - er ____

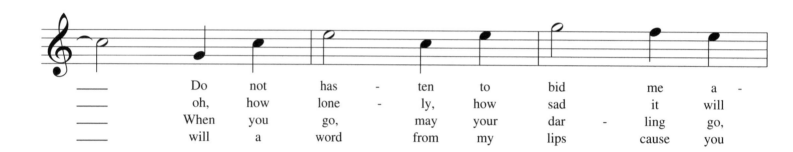

____ Do not has - ten to bid me a -
____ oh, how lone - ly, how sad it will
____ When you go, may your dar - ling go,
____ will a word from my lips cause you

dieu. ____ But re - mem - ber the
be. ____ Oh, ____ think of the
too? ____ Would you leave her be -
pain. ____ And my life, it will

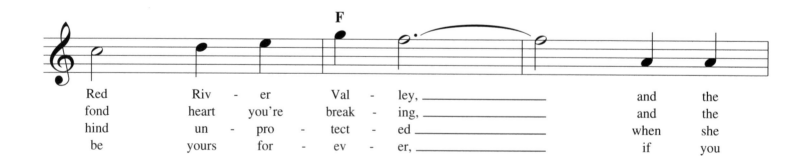

Red Riv - er Val - ley, ____ and the
fond heart you're break - ing, ____ and the
hind un - pro - tect - ed ____ when she
be yours for - ev - er, ____ if you

cow - boy that loves you so true. ____
grief you are caus - ing ____ me. ____
loves no ____ oth - er but you? ____
on - ly will love me a - gain. ____

RING AROUND THE ROSIE

Traditional

Broadly

Ring a - round the ros - y, a pock - et full of po - sies;

ash - es, ash - es, we all fall down.

Lit - tle Sal - ly Wa - ters, sit - ting in a sauc - er,

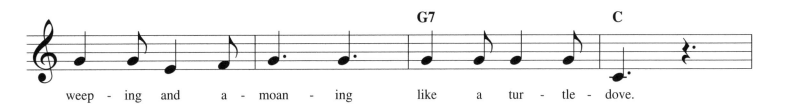

weep - ing and a - moan - ing like a tur - tle - dove.

Rise, Sal - ly rise, _____ wipe your weep - ing eyes; _____

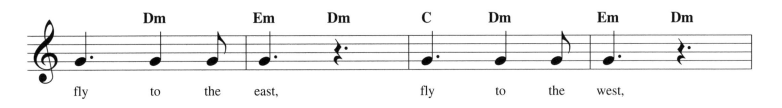

fly to the east, fly to the west,

fly to the one that _____ you love best.

ROCK-A-BYE, BABY

Traditional American Lullaby

Gently

Rock - a - bye, ba - by, on the tree

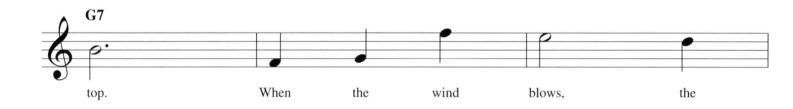

top. When the wind blows, the

cra - dle will rock. When the bough

breaks, the cra - dle will fall, and

down will come ba - by, cra - dle and all.

SAILING, SAILING

Words and Music by
GODFREY MARKS

Briskly

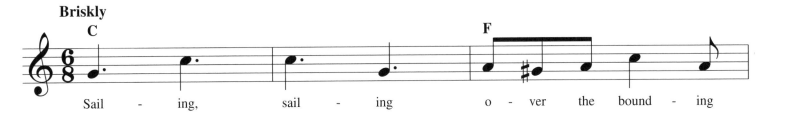

Sail - ing, sail - ing o - ver the bound - ing

main, _____ for man - y a storm - y wind shall blow ere

Jack __ comes home a - gain! _____ Sail - ing, sail - ing

o - ver the bound - ing main, _____ for man - y a storm - y

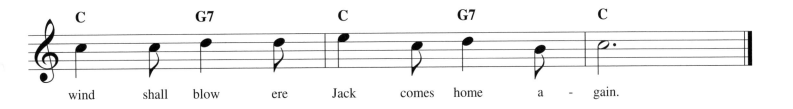

wind shall blow ere Jack comes home a - gain.

SAILOR'S HORNPIPE

Sea Chantey

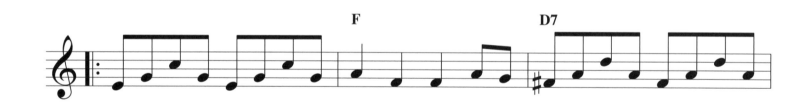

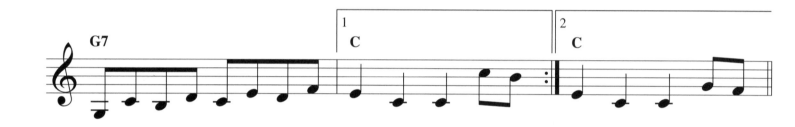

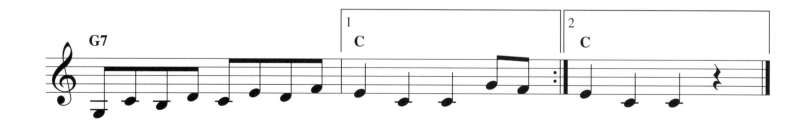

SAKURA
(Cherry Blossoms)

Traditional Japanese Folksong

Gently

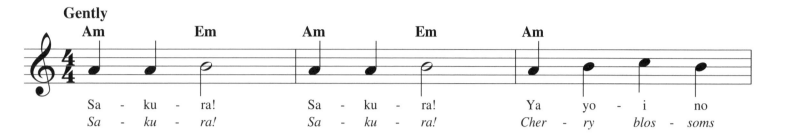

Sa - ku - ra!   Sa - ku - ra!   Ya yo - i   no
Sa - ku - ra!   Sa - ku - ra!   Cher - ry   blos - soms

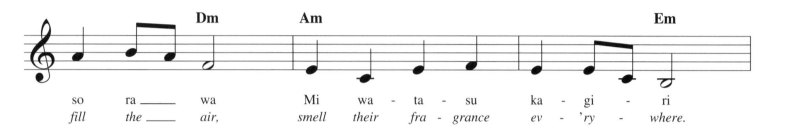

so   ra ____ wa   Mi wa - ta - su ka - gi - ri
fill   the ____ air,   smell their   fra - grance   ev - 'ry - where.

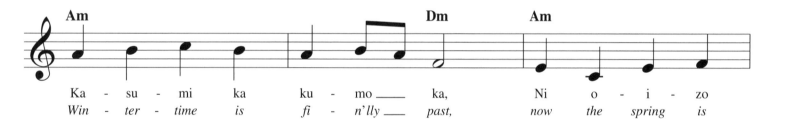

Ka - su - mi ka   ku - mo ____ ka,   Ni   o - i - zo
Win - ter - time is   fi - n'lly ____ past,   now   the spring is

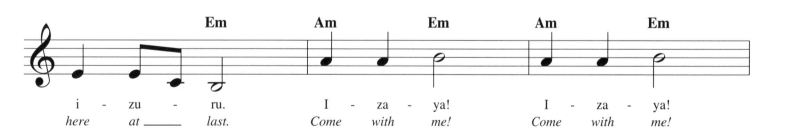

i - zu - ru.   I - za - ya!   I - za - ya!
here   at ____ last.   Come with me!   Come with me!

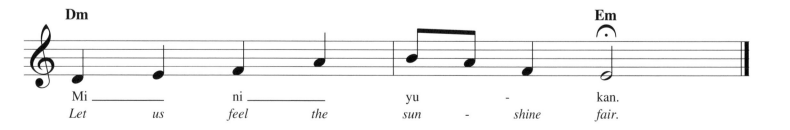

Mi ____ ni ____ yu - kan.
Let   us   feel   the   sun - shine fair.

SANTA LUCIA

By TEODORO COTTRAU

Moderate Waltz

Now 'neath the sil - ver moon o - cean is glow - ing,
When o'er the wa - ters light winds are play - ing,

o'er the calm bil - lows, soft winds are blow - ing.
their spell can soothe __ us, all care al - lay - ing.

Here balm - y breez - es blow, pure joys in - vite __ us,
To thee, sweet Na - po - li, what charms are giv - en,

and as we gen - tly row, all things de - light us.
where smiles cre - a - tion, toil blessed by Heav - en.

Hark! how the sail - ors cry, joy - ous - ly ech - oes nigh,

San - ta __ Lu - ci - a, San - ta Lu - ci - a.

Hark! how the sail - ors cry, joy - ous - ly ech - oes nigh,

San - ta __ Lu - ci - a, San - ta Lu - ci - a.

SCARBOROUGH FAIR

Traditional English

Moderately and freely

1. Are you go - ing to Scar - bor - ough Fair?
2. Have { him / her } make me a cam - bric shirt,
3. Have { him / her } wash it in yon - der dry well,

4.-6. *(See additional lyrics)*

Pars - ley, sage, rose - mar - y and
pars - ley, sage, rose - mar - y and
pars - ley, sage, rose - mar - y and

thyme.   Re - mem - ber me to
thyme.   With - out a seam or
thyme.   Where ne'er a drop of

one who lives there, _____ for once { he / she }
fine nee - dle - work, _____ and then { he'll / she'll }
wa - ter e'er fell, _____ and then { he'll / she'll }

was a true love of mine.   mine.
be a true love of mine.
be a true love of mine.

Additional Lyrics

4. Have him (her) find me an acre of land,
   Parsley, sage, rosemary and thyme.
   Between the sea and over the sand,
   And then he'll (she'll) be a true love of mine.

5. Plow the land with the horn of a lamb,
   Parsley, sage, rosemary and thyme.
   Then sow some seeds from north of the dam,
   And then he'll (she'll) be a true love of mine.

6. If he (she) tells me he (she) can't, I'll reply:
   Parsley, sage, rosemary and thyme.
   Let me know that at least he (she) will try,
   And then he'll (she'll) be a true love of mine.

SCHOOL DAYS
(When We Were a Couple of Kids)

Words by WILL D. COBB
Music by GUS EDWARDS

Waltz tempo

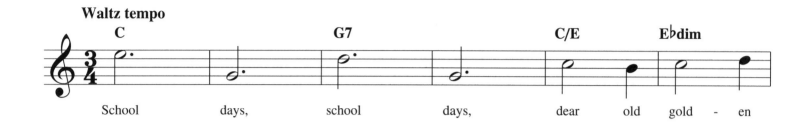

School days, school days, dear old gold - en

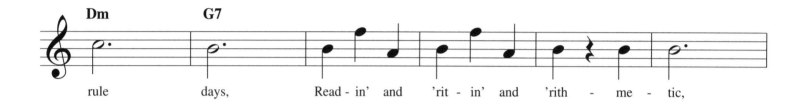

rule days, Read - in' and 'rit - in' and 'rith - me - tic,

Taught to the tune of a hick - 'ry stick. You were my

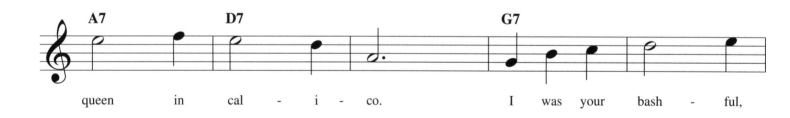

queen in cal - i - co. I was your bash - ful,

bare - foot beau, And you wrote on my slate, "I love you,

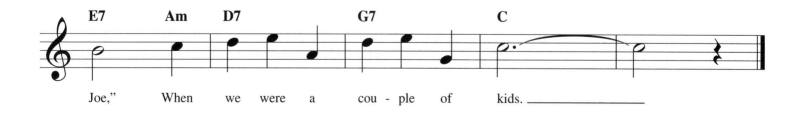

Joe," When we were a cou - ple of kids. _____

SHE'LL BE COMIN' 'ROUND THE MOUNTAIN

Traditional

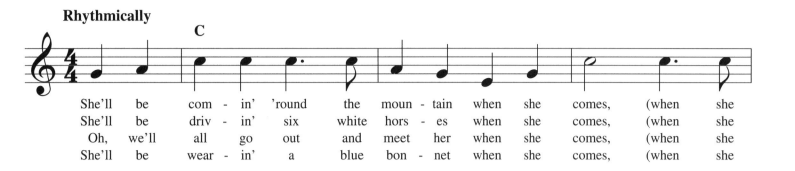

She'll be com - in' 'round the moun - tain when she comes, (when she
She'll be driv - in' six white hors - es when she comes, (when she
Oh, we'll all go out and meet her when she comes, (when she
She'll be wear - in' a blue bon - net when she comes, (when she

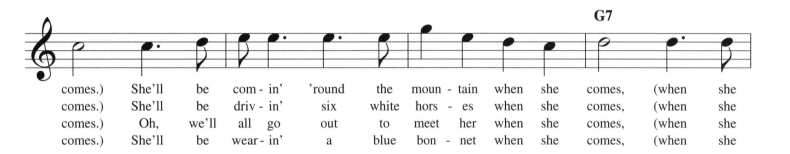

comes.) She'll be com - in' 'round the moun - tain when she comes, (when she
comes.) She'll be driv - in' six white hors - es when she comes, (when she
comes.) Oh, we'll all go out to meet her when she comes, (when she
comes.) She'll be wear - in' a blue bon - net when she comes, (when she

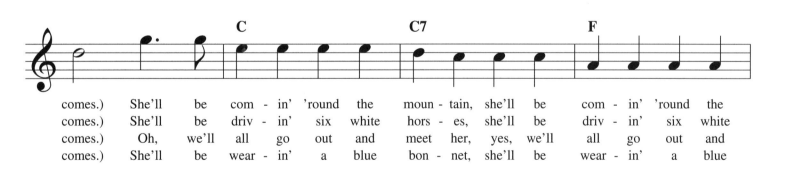

comes.) She'll be com - in' 'round the moun - tain, she'll be com - in' 'round the
comes.) She'll be driv - in' six white hors - es, she'll be driv - in' six white
comes.) Oh, we'll all go out and meet her, yes, we'll all go out and
comes.) She'll be wear - in' a blue bon - net, she'll be wear - in' a blue

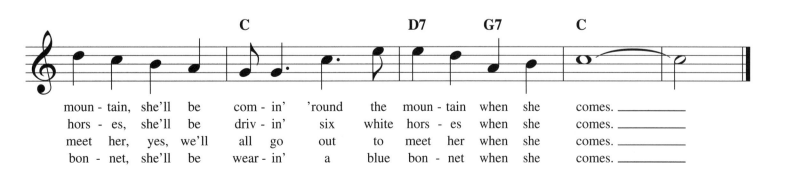

moun - tain, she'll be com - in' 'round the moun - tain when she comes. _____
hors - es, she'll be driv - in' six white hors - es when she comes. _____
meet her, yes, we'll all go out to meet her when she comes. _____
bon - net, she'll be wear - in' a blue bon - net when she comes. _____

SHE WORE A YELLOW RIBBON

Words and Music by
GEORGE A. NORTON

Briskly

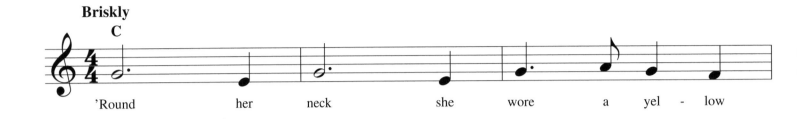

'Round her neck she wore a yel - low

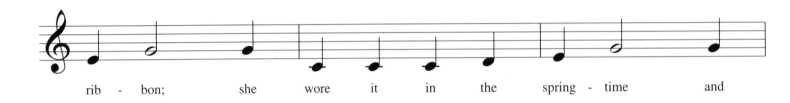

rib - bon; she wore it in the spring - time and

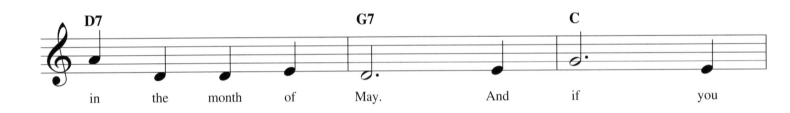

in the month of May. And if you

asked her why the heck she wore it, she

says, "It's for my lov - er who is far, far a -

way." Far a - way, _____ far a - way. _____

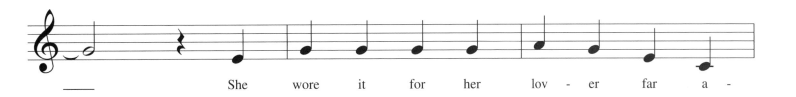

____ She wore it for her lov - er far a -

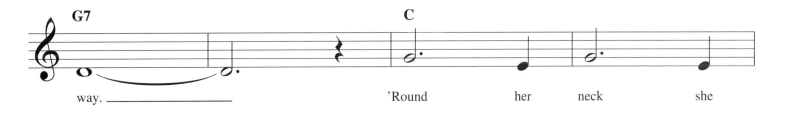

way. _____ 'Round her neck she

wore a yel - low rib - bon; she wore it for her

lov - er who is far, far a - way.

SHENANDOAH

American Folksong

Gently

Oh, Shen - an - doah, _____ I long to hear you. _____ } A -
Oh, Shen - an - doah, _____ I love your daugh - ter. _____
Oh, Shen - an - doah, _____ I'm bound to leave you. _____

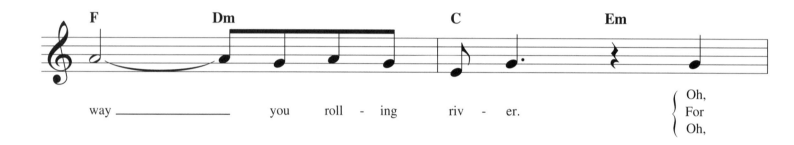

way _____ you roll - ing riv - er. { Oh,
For
Oh,

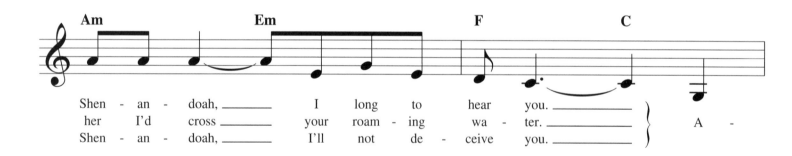

Shen - an - doah, _____ I long to hear you. _____ } A -
her I'd cross _____ your roam - ing wa - ter. _____
Shen - an - doah, _____ I'll not de - ceive you. _____

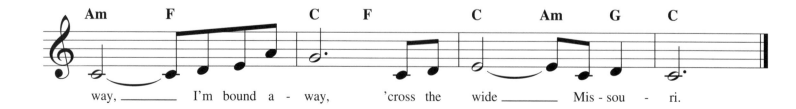

way, _____ I'm bound a - way, 'cross the wide _____ Mis - sou - ri.

SHOO FLY, DON'T BOTHER ME

Words by BILLY REEVES
Music by FRANK CAMPBELL

Moderately

Shoo, fly, don't both - er me. Shoo, fly, don't

both - er me. Shoo, fly, don't both - er me, for

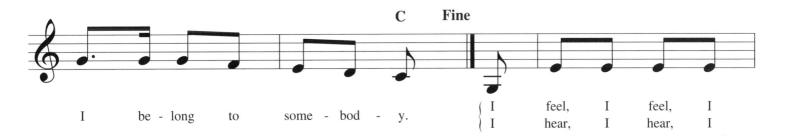

I be - long to some - bod - y.

I feel, I feel, I
I hear, I hear, I

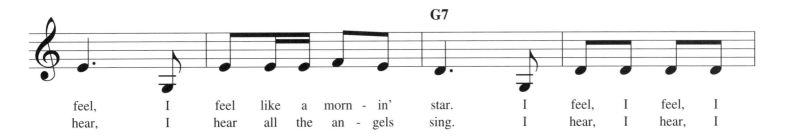

feel, I feel like a morn - in' star. I feel, I feel, I
hear, I hear all the an - gels sing. I hear, I hear, I

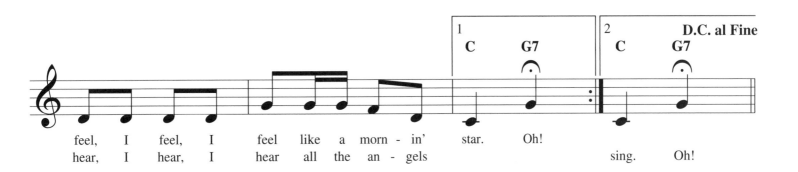

feel, I feel, I feel like a morn - in' star. Oh!
hear, I hear, I hear all the an - gels sing. Oh!

SHORT'NIN' BREAD

Plantation Song

Moderately

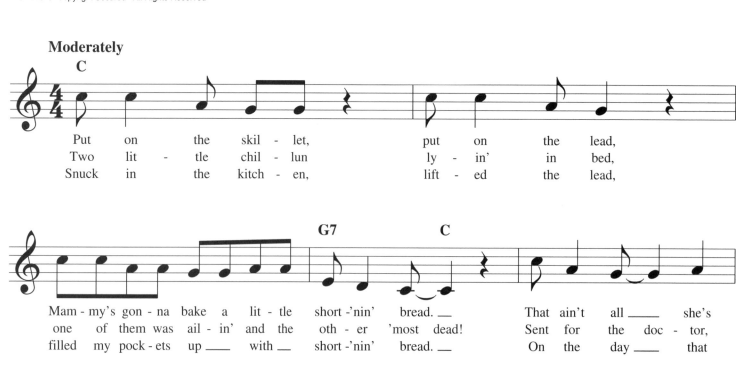

Put on the skil - let, put on the lead,
Two lit - tle chil - lun ly - in' in bed,
Snuck in the kitch - en, lift - ed the lead,

Mam - my's gon - na bake a lit - tle short -'nin' bread. __ That ain't all ____ she's
one of them was ail - in' and the oth - er 'most dead! Sent for the doc - tor,
filled my pock - ets up ____ with __ short -'nin' bread. __ On the day ____ that

gon - na do, ____ Mam - my's gon - na make a pot of cof - fee, too. ____
doc - tor said, __ got to feed them chil - lun some __ short -'nin' bread. __
I get wed, __ hope to have a gal who's good at short -'nin' bread. __

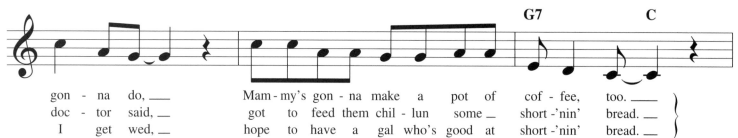

Mam - my's lit - tle ba - by loves short -'nin', short -'nin', Mam - my's lit - tle ba - by loves

short -'nin' bread. __ Mam - my's lit - tle ba - by loves short -'nin', short -'nin',

1, 2.

3.

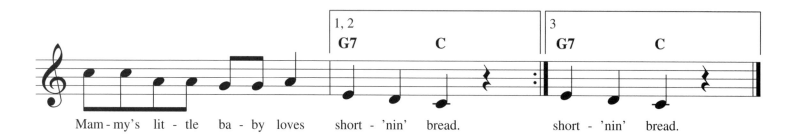

Mam - my's lit - tle ba - by loves short -'nin' bread. short -'nin' bread.

SIMPLE GIFTS

Traditional Shaker Hymn

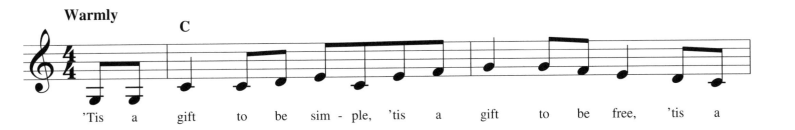

'Tis a gift to be sim - ple, 'tis a gift to be free, 'tis a

gift to come down where you ought to be, and

when we find our - selves in the place just right, 'twill be in the val - ley of

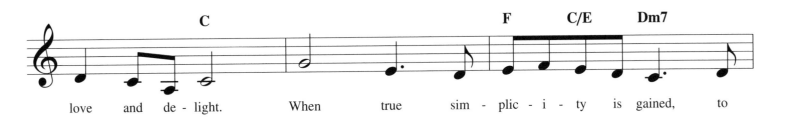

love and de - light. When true sim - plic - i - ty is gained, to

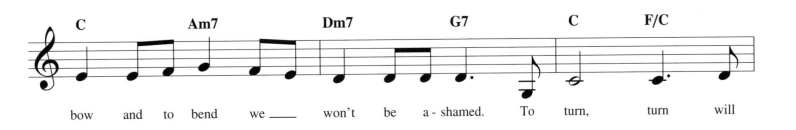

bow and to bend we ___ won't be a - shamed. To turn, turn will

be our de - light till by turn - ing and turn - ing we come out right.

SING A SONG OF SIXPENCE

Traditional

With motion

Sing a song of six - pence, a pock - et full of rye;

four and twen - ty black - birds baked in a pie.

When the pie was o - pened, the birds be - gan to sing.

Was - n't that a dain - ty dish to set be - fore a king? The

king was in the count - ing - house, count - ing out his mon - ey. The

queen was in the par - lor, eat - ing bread and hon - ey. The

maid was in the gar - den, hang - ing out the clothes. A -

long ___ came a black - bird and pecked ___ off her nose.

SKIP TO MY LOU

Traditional

Joyfully

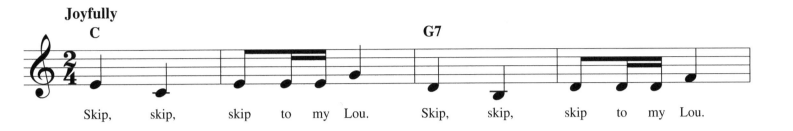

Skip, skip, skip to my Lou. Skip, skip, skip to my Lou.

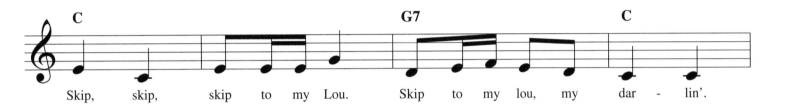

Skip, skip, skip to my Lou. Skip to my lou, my dar - lin'.

Flies in the but - ter - milk, shoo, shoo, shoo! Flies in the but - ter - milk,
Lost my part - ner, what'll I do? Lost my part - ner,
I'll get an - oth - er one, purtier than you. I'll get an - oth - er one,
Can't get a red bird, a blue - bird -'ll do. Can't get a red bird, a

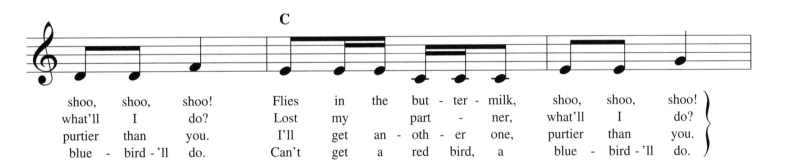

shoo, shoo, shoo! Flies in the but - ter - milk, shoo, shoo, shoo!
what'll I do? Lost my part - ner, what'll I do?
purtier than you. I'll get an - oth - er one, purtier than you.
blue - bird -'ll do. Can't get a red bird, a blue - bird -'ll do.

Skip to my Lou, my dar - lin'.

SIYAHAMBA
(We Are Marching in the Light of God)

African Folksong

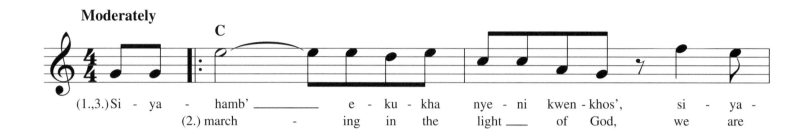

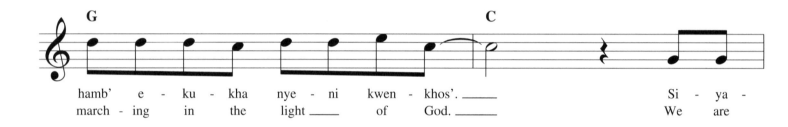

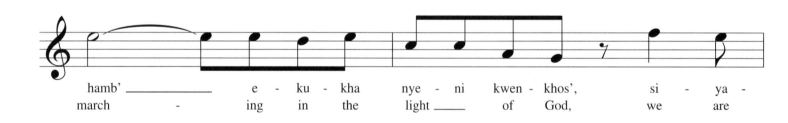

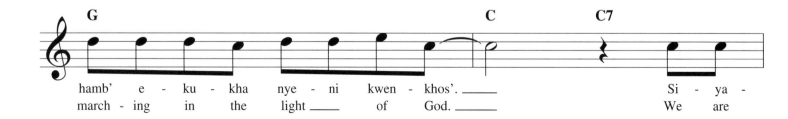

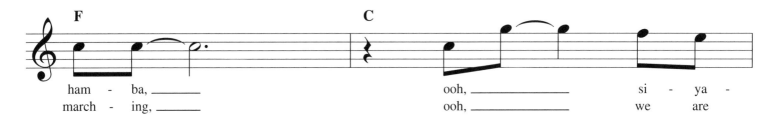

hamba, _____ ooh, _____ si - ya -
march - ing, _____ ooh, _____ we are

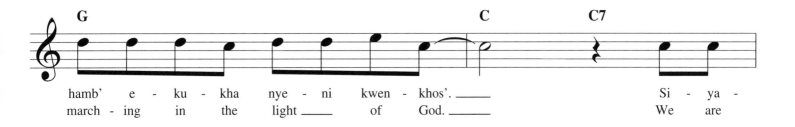

hamb' e - ku - kha nye - ni kwen - khos'. _____ Si - ya -
march - ing in the light ____ of God. _____ We are

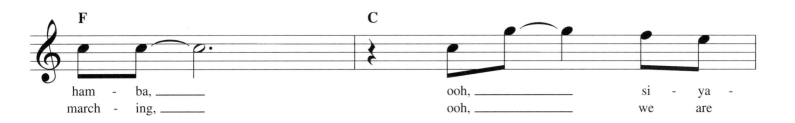

hamba, _____ ooh, _____ si - ya -
march - ing, _____ ooh, _____ we are

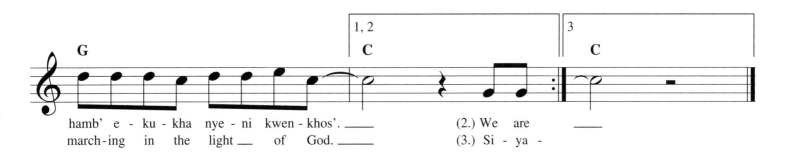

hamb' e - ku - kha nye - ni kwen - khos'. ____ (2.) We are ____
march - ing in the light ___ of God. ____ (3.) Si - ya -

Pronunciation Guide

Siyahamba = see-yah-hahm-bah
Ekukha = eh-koo-kah
Nyeni = n͜yeh-nee
Kwenkhos' = kwehn-kōs

SONG OF THE VOLGA BOATMAN

Russian Folksong

THE STREETS OF LAREDO

American Cowboy Song

SWEET BETSY FROM PIKE

American Folksong

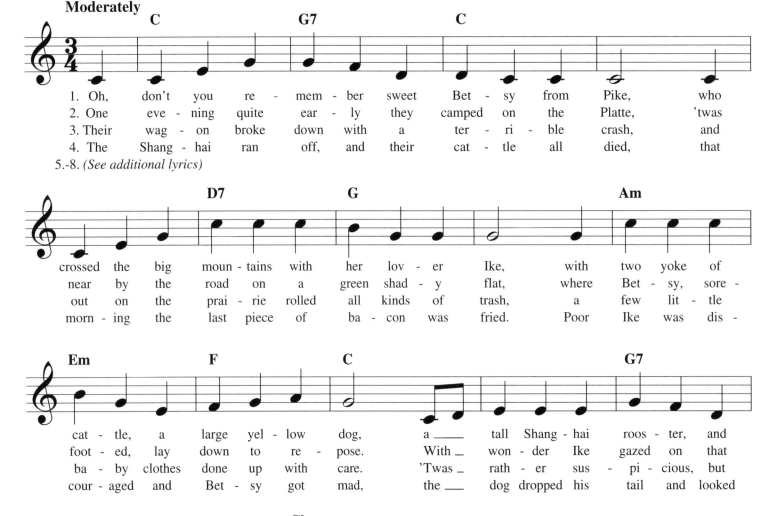

Moderately

1. Oh, don't you re - mem - ber sweet Bet - sy from Pike, who
2. One eve - ning quite ear - ly they camped on the Platte, 'twas
3. Their wag - on broke down with a ter - ri - ble crash, and
4. The Shang - hai ran off, and their cat - tle all died, that

5.-8. *(See additional lyrics)*

crossed the big moun - tains with her lov - er Ike, with two yoke of
near by the road on a green shad - y flat, where Bet - sy, sore -
out on the prai - rie rolled all kinds of trash, a few lit - tle
morn - ing the last piece of ba - con was fried. Poor Ike was dis -

cat - tle, a large yel - low dog, a ___ tall Shang - hai roos - ter, and
foot - ed, lay down to re - pose. With _ won - der Ike gazed on that
ba - by clothes done up with care. 'Twas _ rath - er sus - pi - cious, but
cour - aged and Bet - sy got mad, the ___ dog dropped his tail and looked

Chorus

one spot - ted hog.
Pike Coun - ty rose.
all on the square.
won - drous - ly sad.

Say - ing good - bye, Pike Coun - ty, fare - well for a

while. We'll _ come back a - gain when we've panned out our pile.

Additional Lyrics

5. They soon reached the desert where Betsy gave out,
And down in the sand she lay rolling about,
While Ike, half distracted, looked on with surprise.
Saying, "Betsy, get up. You'll get sand in your eyes."
Chorus

6. Sweet Betsy got up in a great deal of pain,
Declared she'd go back to Pike County again,
But Ike gave a sigh, and they fondly embraced
And they traveled along with his arm 'round her waist.
Chorus

7. They suddenly stopped on a very high hill,
With wonder looked down upon old Placerville;
Ike sighed when he said, and he cast his eyes down,
"Sweet Betsy, my darling, we've got to Hangtown."
Chorus

8. Long Ike and sweet Betsy attended a dance;
Ike wore a pair of his Pike County pants;
Sweet Betsy was dressed up in ribbons and rings;
Says Ike, "You're an angel, but where are your wings?"
Chorus

TAKE ME OUT TO THE BALL GAME

Words by JACK NORWORTH
Music by ALBERT VON TILZER

THREE BLIND MICE

Traditional

Briskly

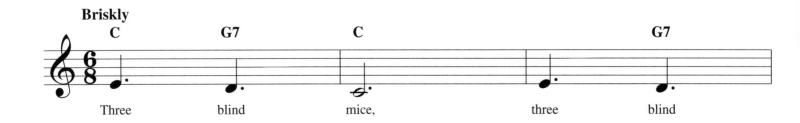

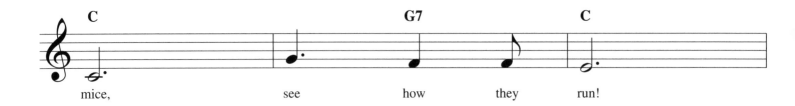

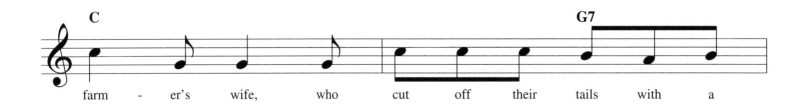

'TIS THE LAST ROSE OF SUMMER

Words by THOMAS MOORE
Music by RICHARD ALFRED MILLIKEN

Reflectively

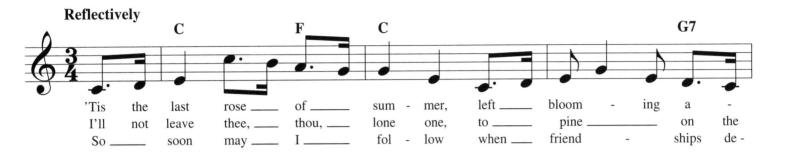

'Tis the last rose ____ of ____ sum - mer, left ____ bloom - ing a -
I'll not leave thee, ____ thou, ____ lone one, to ____ pine ____ on the
So ____ soon may ____ I ____ fol - low when ____ friend - ships de -

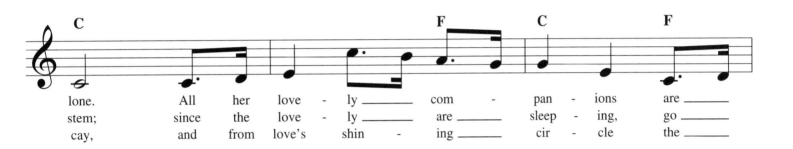

lone. All her love - ly ____ com - pan - ions are ____
stem; since the love - ly ____ are ____ sleep - ing, go ____
cay, and from love's shin - ing ____ cir - cle the ____

fad - ed and ____ gone. No ____ flow - er of her
sleep ____ thou with them. Thus ____ kind - ly I'll
gems ____ drop a - way. When ____ true ____ hearts lie

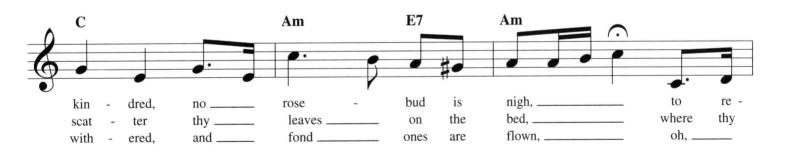

kin - dred, no ____ rose - bud is nigh, ____ to re -
scat - ter thy ____ leaves ____ on the bed, ____ where thy
with - ered, and ____ fond ____ ones are flown, ____ oh, ____

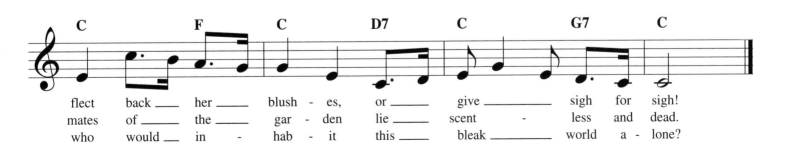

flect back ____ her ____ blush - es, or ____ give ____ sigh for sigh!
mates of ____ the ____ gar - den lie ____ scent - less and dead.
who would ____ in - hab - it this ____ bleak ____ world a - lone?

TOM DOOLEY

Traditional Folksong

TURKEY IN THE STRAW

American Folksong

Lively

As ___ I was a - go - ing on ___ down the road, with a
Went ___ out to ___ milk ___ and I did - n't know how, I ___

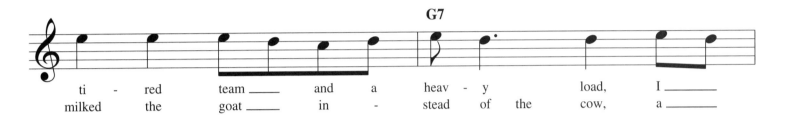

ti - red team ___ and a heav - y load, I ___
milked the goat ___ in - stead of the cow, a ___

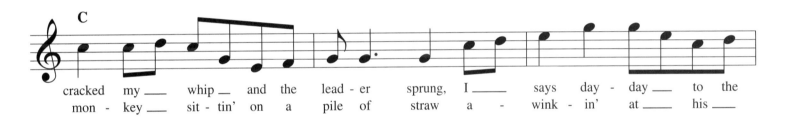

cracked my ___ whip ___ and the lead - er sprung, I ___ says day - day ___ to the
mon - key ___ sit - tin' on a pile of straw a - wink - in' at ___ his ___

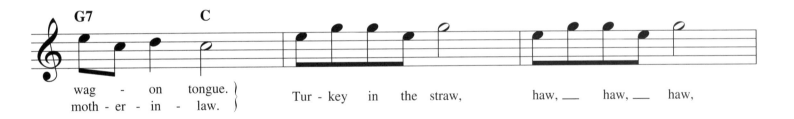

wag - on tongue.)
moth - er - in - law.)   Tur - key in the straw, haw, ___ haw, ___ haw,

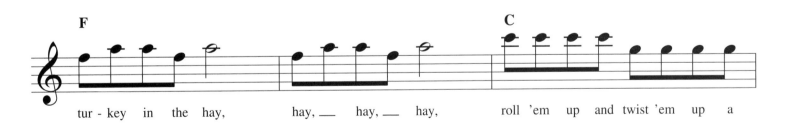

tur - key in the hay, hay, ___ hay, ___ hay, roll 'em up and twist 'em up a

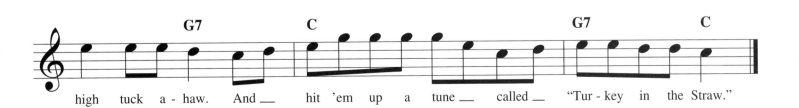

high tuck a - haw. And ___ hit 'em up a tune ___ called ___ "Tur - key in the Straw."

THE WABASH CANNON BALL

American Hobo Song, circa 1880s

Briskly

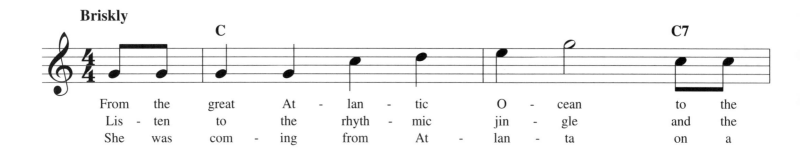

From the great At - lan - tic O - cean to the
Lis - ten to the rhyth - mic jin - gle and the
She was com - ing from At - lan - ta on a

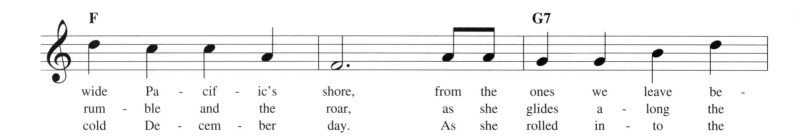

wide Pa - cif - ic's shore, from the ones we leave be -
rum - ble and the roar, as she glides a - long the
cold De - cem - ber day. As she rolled in - to the

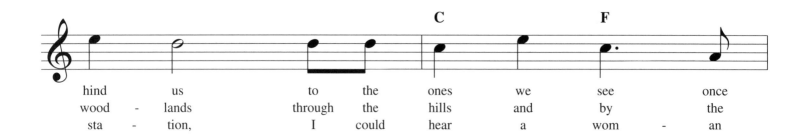

hind us to the ones we see once
wood - lands through the hills and by the
sta - tion, I could hear a wom - an

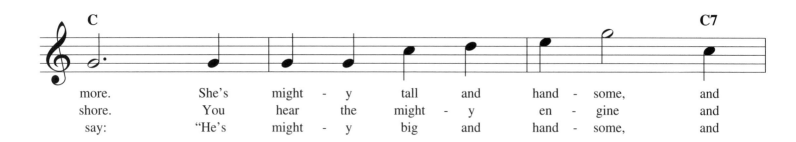

more. She's might - y tall and hand - some, and
shore. You hear the might - y en - gine and
say: "He's might - y big and hand - some, and

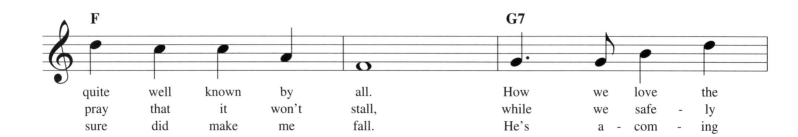

quite well known by all. How we love the
pray that it won't stall, while we safe - ly
sure did make me fall. He's a - com - ing

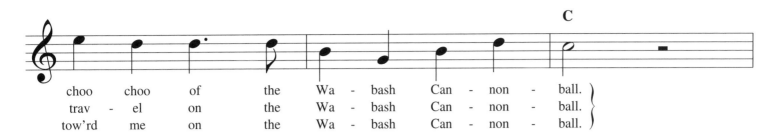

choo choo of the Wa - bash Can - non - ball.
trav - el on the Wa - bash Can - non - ball.
tow'rd me on the Wa - bash Can - non - ball.

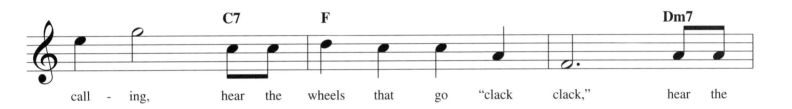

Hear the bell and whis - tle

call - ing, hear the wheels that go "clack clack," hear the

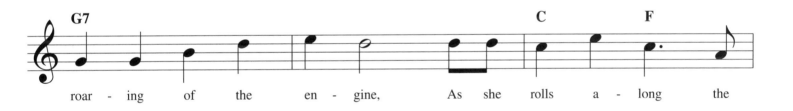

roar - ing of the en - gine, As she rolls a - long the

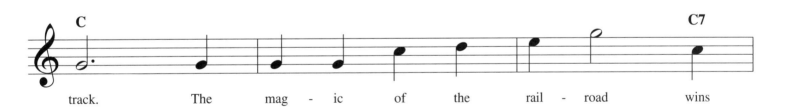

track. The mag - ic of the rail - road wins

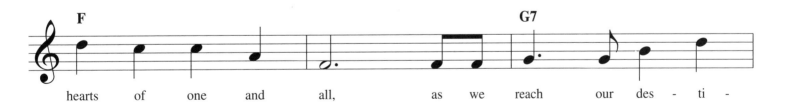

hearts of one and all, as we reach our des - ti -

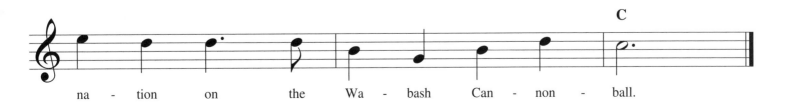

na - tion on the Wa - bash Can - non - ball.

WAYFARING STRANGER

Southern American Folk Hymn

I am a poor _____ way-far-ing stran-ger, while trav-'ling through _____ this world of
I know dark clouds _____ will gath-er 'round me, I know my way _____ is rough and
I'll soon be free _____ from ev-'ry tri-al, my bod-y sleep _____ in the church-

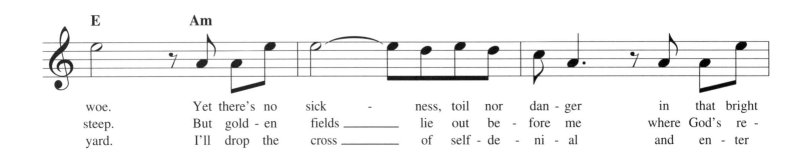

woe. Yet there's no sick - ness, toil nor dan-ger in that bright
steep. But gold-en fields _____ lie out be-fore me where God's re-
yard. I'll drop the cross _____ of self-de - ni - al and en-ter

world _____ to which I go. I'm go-ing there _____ to see my
deemed _____ shall ev-er sleep. I'm go-ing there _____ to see my
on _____ my great re-ward. I'm go-ing there _____ to see my

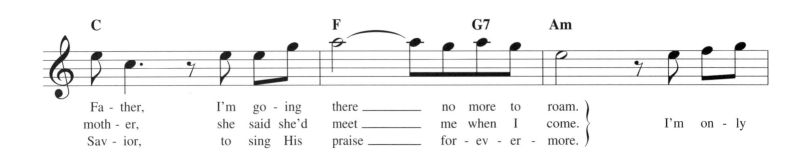

Fa - ther, I'm go-ing there _____ no more to roam.
moth-er, she said she'd meet _____ me when I come.   I'm on-ly
Sav - ior, to sing His praise _____ for-ev-er-more.

go - ing o-ver Jor-dan, I'm on-ly go - ing o-ver home.

WHEN JOHNNY COMES MARCHING HOME

Words and Music by
PATRICK SARSFIELD GILMORE

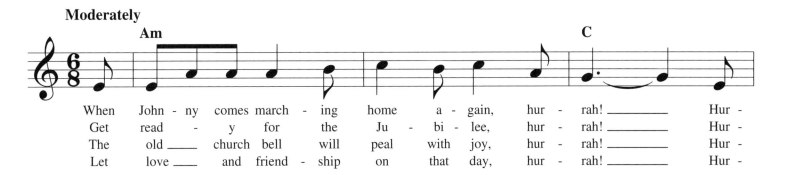

When John - ny comes march - ing home a - gain, hur - rah! _____ Hur -
Get read - y for the Ju - bi - lee, hur - rah! _____ Hur -
The old ___ church bell will peal with joy, hur - rah! _____ Hur -
Let love ___ and friend - ship on that day, hur - rah! _____ Hur -

rah! _____ We'll give him a heart - y wel - come then, hur -
rah! _____ We'll give ___ the he - ro three times three, hur -
rah! _____ To wel - come home our dar - ling boy, hur -
rah! _____ Their choic - est treas - ures then dis - play, hur -

rah! _____ Hur - rah! _____ Oh, the men will cheer and the
rah! _____ Hur - rah! _____ The ___ lau - rel wreath ___ is
rah! _____ Hur - rah! _____ The ___ vil - lage lads ___ and
rah! _____ Hur - rah! _____ And ___ let each one ___ per -

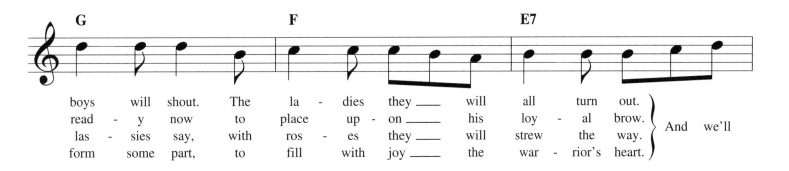

boys will shout. The la - dies they ___ will all turn out.
read - y now to place up - on ___ his loy - al brow.   And we'll
las - sies say, with ros - es they ___ will strew the way.
form some part, to fill with joy ___ the war - rior's heart.

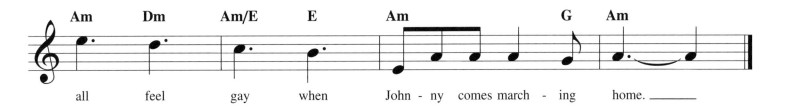

all feel gay when John - ny comes march - ing home. _____

WHEN THE SAINTS GO MARCHING IN

Words by KATHERINE E. PURVIS
Music by JAMES M. BLACK

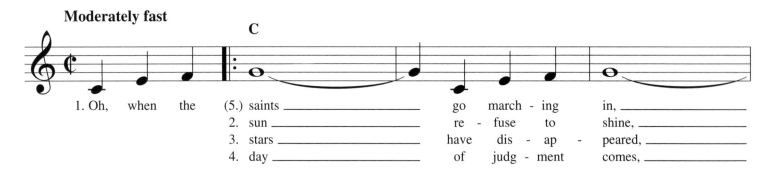

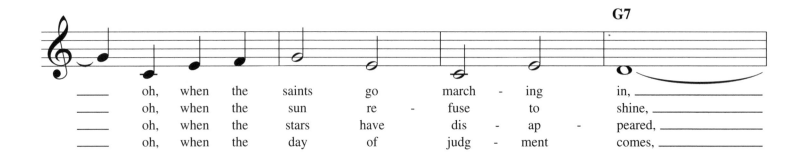

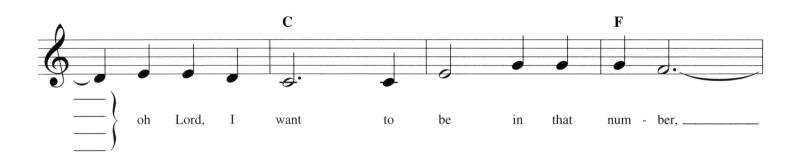

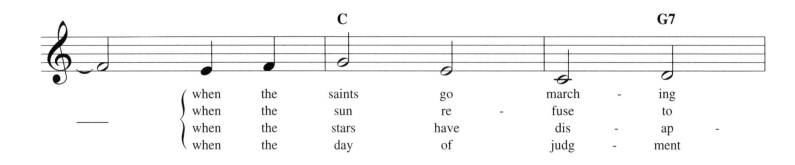

WILL THE CIRCLE BE UNBROKEN

Words by ADA R. HABERSHON
Music by CHARLES H. GABRIEL

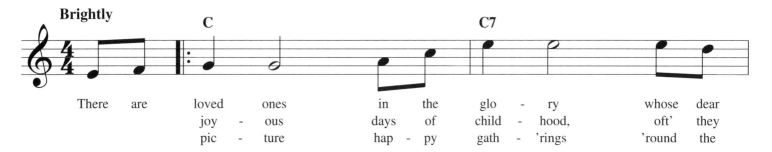

Brightly

There are loved ones in the glo - ry whose dear
joy - ous days of child - hood, whose oft' they
pic - ture hap - py gath - 'rings 'round the

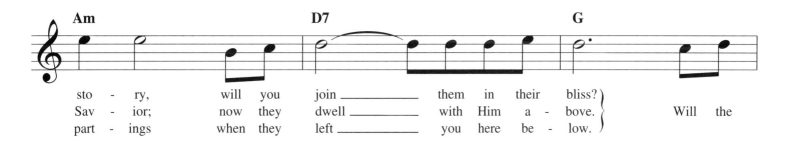

forms _____ you of - ten miss; when you close your earth - ly
told _____ of won - drous love, point - ed to the dy - ing
fire - side long a - go, and you think of tear - ful

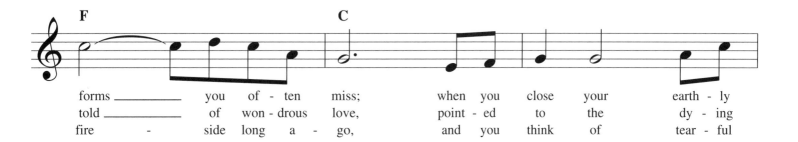

sto - ry, will you join _____ them in their bliss?
Sav - ior; now they dwell _____ with Him a - bove. Will the
part - ings when they left _____ you here be - low.

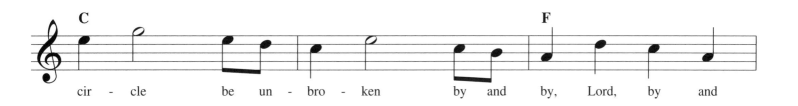

cir - cle be un - bro - ken by and by, Lord, by and

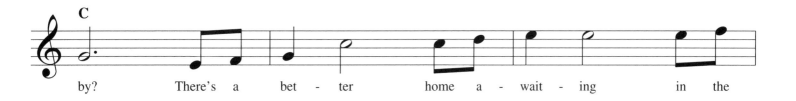

by? There's a bet - ter home a - wait - ing in the

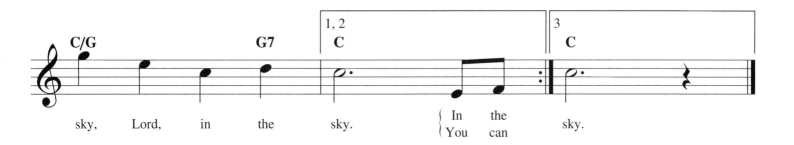

sky, Lord, in the sky.

1, 2
In the sky.
You can

3
sky.

WORRIED MAN BLUES

Traditional

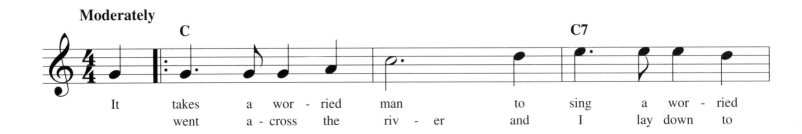

It takes a wor - ried man to sing a wor - ried
went a - cross the riv - er and I lay down to

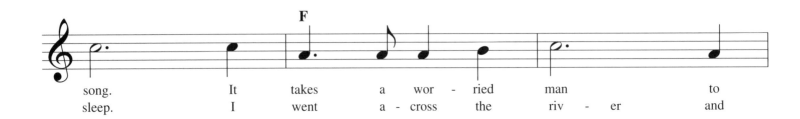

song. It takes a wor - ried man to
sleep. I went a - cross the riv - er to and

sing a wor - ried song. It takes a wor - ried man to
I lay down to sleep. I went a - cross the riv - er and

sing a wor - ried song. I'm wor - ried now, but I
I lay down to sleep. When I woke up, had

won't be wor - ried long. I
shack - les on my feet.

YANKEE DOODLE

Traditional

Moderately fast

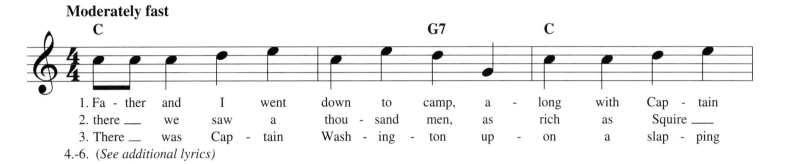

1. Fa - ther and I went down to camp, a - long with Cap - tain
2. there __ we saw a thou - sand men, as rich as Squire __
3. There __ was Cap - tain Wash - ing - ton up - on a slap - ping

4.-6. *(See additional lyrics)*

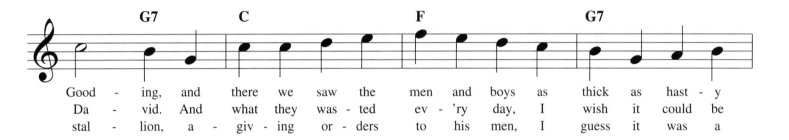

Good - ing, and there we saw the men and boys as thick as hast - y
Da - vid. And what they was - ted ev - 'ry day, I wish it could be
stal - lion, a - giv - ing or - ders to his men, I guess it was a

pud - ding.
saved. __   Yan - kee Doo - dle, keep it up, Yan - kee Doo - dle dan - dy. Mind the mu - sic
mil - lion.

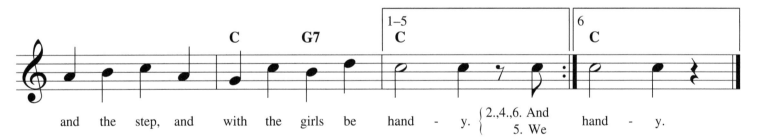

and the step, and with the girls be hand - y.   { 2.,4.,6. And   hand - y.
                                                  { 5. We

Additional Lyrics

4. And then the feathers on his hat,
   They looked so 'tarnel fine, ah!
   I wanted peskily to get
   To give to me Jemima.

5. We saw a little barrel, too,
   The heads were made of leather.
   They knocked on it with little clubs
   And called the folks together.

6. And there they'd fife away like fun,
   And play on cornstalk fiddles.
   And some had ribbons red as blood
   All bound around their middles.

THE YELLOW ROSE OF TEXAS

Words and Music by
J.K., 1858

Moderately

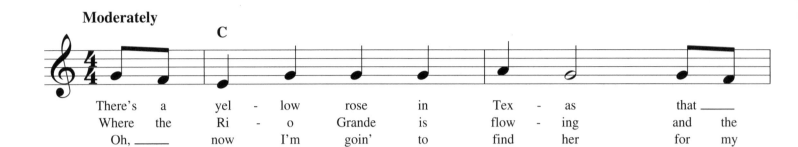

There's a yel - low rose in Tex - as that _____
Where the Ri - o Grande is flow - ing and the
Oh, _____ now I'm goin' to find her for my

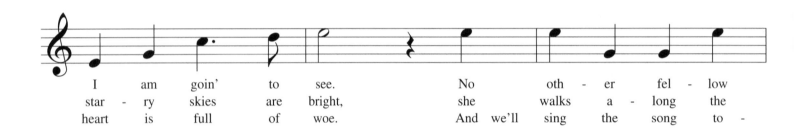

I am goin' to see. No oth - er fel - low
star - ry skies are bright, she walks a - long the
heart is full of woe. And we'll sing the song to -

loves her, no - bod - y, on - ly me. She
riv - er in the qui - et sum - mer night. She
geth - er, that we sang so long a - go. We'll

cried so when I left her, it _____ like to broke my
thinks, if I re - mem - ber, when we part - ed long a -
play the ban - jo gai - ly and we'll sing the songs of

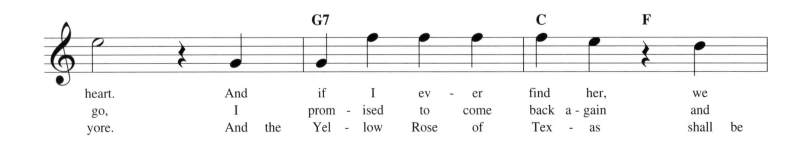

heart. And if I ev - er find her, we
go, I prom - ised to come back a - gain and
yore. And the Yel - low Rose of Tex - as shall be

nev - er - more will part.
not to leave her so. }
mine for - ev - er - more. }
She's the sweet - est rose of

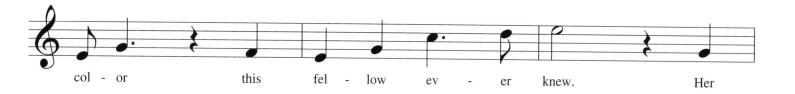

col - or this fel - low ev - er knew. Her

eyes are bright as dia - monds, they spar - kle like the

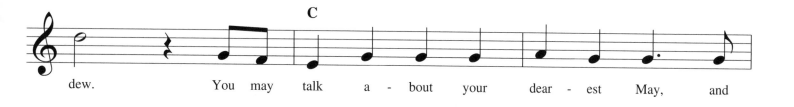

dew. You may talk a - bout your dear - est May, and

sing of Ro - sa Lee. But the Yel - low Rose of

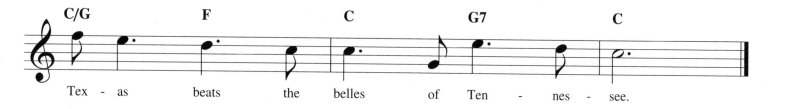

Tex - as beats the belles of Ten - nes - see.

CHORD SPELLER

C chords

C	C–E–G
Cm	C–E♭–G
C7	C–E–G–B♭
Cdim	C–E♭–G♭
C+	C–E–G♯

C♯ or D♭ chords

C♯	C♯–F–G♯
C♯m	C♯–E–G♯
C♯7	C♯–F– G♯–B
C♯dim	C♯–E–G
C♯+	C♯–F–A

D chords

D	D–F♯–A
Dm	D–F–A
D7	D–F♯–A–C
Ddim	D–F–A♭
D+	D–F♯–A♯

E♭ chords

E♭	E♭–G–B♭
E♭m	E♭–G♭–B♭
E♭7	E♭–G–B♭–D♭
E♭dim	E♭–G♭–A
E♭+	E♭–G–B

E chords

E	E–G♯–B
Em	E–G–B
E7	E–G♯–B–D
Edim	E–G–B♭
E+	E–G♯–C

F chords

F	F–A–C
Fm	F–A♭–C
F7	F–A–C–E♭
Fdim	F–A♭–B
F+	F–A–C♯

F♯ or G♭ chords

F♯	F♯–A♯–C♯
F♯m	F♯–A–C♯
F♯7	F♯–A♯–C♯–E
F♯dim	F♯–A–C
F♯+	F♯–A♯–D

G chords

G	G–B–D
Gm	G–B♭–D
G7	G–B–D–F
Gdim	G–B♭–D♭
G+	G–B–D♯

G♯ or A♭ chords

A♭	A♭–C–E♭
A♭m	A♭–B–E♭
A♭7	A♭–C–E♭–G♭
A♭dim	A♭–B–D
A♭+	A♭–C–E

A chords

A	A–C♯–E
Am	A–C–E
A7	A–C♯–E–G
Adim	A–C–E♭
A+	A–C♯–F

B♭ chords

B♭	B♭–D–F
B♭m	B♭–D♭–F
B♭7	B♭–D–F–A♭
B♭dim	B♭–D♭–E
B♭+	B♭–D–F♯

B chords

B	B–D♯–F♯
Bm	B–D–F♯
B7	B–D♯–F♯–A
Bdim	B–D–F
B+	B–D♯–G

Important Note: A slash chord (C/E, G/B) tells you that a certain bass note is to be played under a particular harmony. In the case of C/E, the chord is C and the bass note is E.

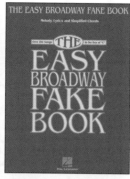

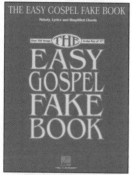
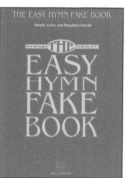

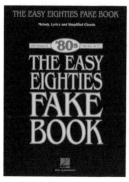
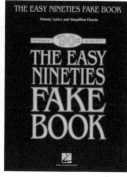

THE ULTIMATE COLLECTION OF
FAKE BOOKS

The Real Book – Sixth Edition

Hal Leonard proudly presents the first legitimate and legal editions of these books ever produced. These bestselling titles are mandatory for anyone who plays jazz! Over 400 songs, including: All By Myself • Dream a Little Dream of Me • God Bless the Child • Like Someone in Love • When I Fall in Love • and more.

00240221 Volume 1, C Edition $29.99
00240224 Volume 1, B♭ Edition $29.99
00240225 Volume 1, E♭ Edition $29.99
00240226 Volume 1, BC Edition $29.95
00240222 Volume 2, C Edition $29.95
00240227 Volume 2, B♭ Edition $29.95
00240228 Volume 2, E♭ Edition $29.95

Best Fake Book Ever – 3rd Edition

More than 1,000 songs from all styles of music, including: All My Loving • At the Hop • Cabaret • Dust in the Wind • Fever • From a Distance • Hello, Dolly! • Hey Jude • King of the Road • Longer • Misty • Route 66 • Sentimental Journey • Somebody • Song Sung Blue • Spinning Wheel • Unchained Melody • We Will Rock You • What a Wonderful World • Wooly Bully • Y.M.C.A. • and more.

00290239 C Edition $49.99
00240083 B♭ Edition $49.95
00240084 E♭ Edition $49.95

Classic Rock Fake Book – 2nd Edition

This fake book is a great compilation of more than 250 terrific songs of the rock era, arranged for piano, voice, guitar and all C instruments. Includes: All Right Now • American Woman • Birthday • Honesty • I Shot the Sheriff • I Want You to Want Me • Imagine • It's Still Rock and Roll to Me • Lay Down Sally • Layla • My Generation • Rock and Roll All Nite • Spinning Wheel • White Room • We Will Rock You • lots more!
00240108 ....$29.95

Classical Fake Book – 2nd Edition

This unprecedented, amazingly comprehensive reference includes over 850 classical themes and melodies for all classical music lovers. Includes everything from Renaissance music to Vivaldi and Mozart to Mendelssohn. Lyrics in the original language are included when appropriate.
00240044 ....$34.95

The Disney Fake Book – 2nd Edition

Over 200 of the most beloved songs of all time, including: Be Our Guest • Can You Feel the Love Tonight • Colors of the Wind • Cruella De Vil • Friend Like Me • Heigh-Ho • It's a Small World • Mickey Mouse March • Supercalifragilisticexpialidocious • Under the Sea • When You Wish upon a Star • A Whole New World • Zip-A-Dee-Doo-Dah • and more!
00240039 ....$27.95

(Disney characters and artwork © Disney Enterprises, Inc.)

The Folksong Fake Book

Over 1,000 folksongs perfect for performers, school teachers, and hobbyists. Includes: Bury Me Not on the Lone Prairie • Clementine • Danny Boy • The Erie Canal • Go, Tell It on the Mountain • Home on the Range • Kumbaya • Michael Row the Boat Ashore • Shenandoah • Simple Gifts • Swing Low, Sweet Chariot • When Johnny Comes Marching Home • Yankee Doodle • and many more.
00240151 ....$24.95

The Hymn Fake Book

Nearly 1,000 multi-denominational hymns perfect for church musicians or hobbyists: Amazing Grace • Christ the Lord Is Risen Today • For the Beauty of the Earth • It Is Well with My Soul • A Mighty Fortress Is Our God • O for a Thousand Tongues to Sing • Praise to the Lord, the Almighty • Take My Life and Let It Be • What a Friend We Have in Jesus • and hundreds more!
00240145 ....$24.95

The Praise & Worship Fake Book

400 songs: As the Deer • Better Is One Day • Come, Now Is the Time to Worship • Firm Foundation • Glorify Thy Name • Here I Am to Worship • I Could Sing of Your Love Forever • Lord, I Lift Your Name on High • More Precious Than Silver • Open the Eyes of My Heart • The Power of Your Love • Shine, Jesus, Shine • Trading My Sorrows • We Fall Down • You Are My All in All • and more.
00240234 $34.95

The R&B Fake Book – 2nd Edition

This terrific fake book features 375 classic R&B hits: Baby Love • Best of My Love • Dancing in the Street • Easy • Get Ready • Heatwave • Here and Now • Just Once • Let's Get It On • The Loco-Motion • (You Make Me Feel Like) A Natural Woman • One Sweet Day • Papa Was a Rollin' Stone • Save the Best for Last • September • Sexual Healing • Shop Around • Still • Tell It Like It Is • Up on the Roof • Walk on By • What's Going On • more!
00240107 C Edition $29.95

Ultimate Broadway Fake Book – 5th Edition

More than 700 show-stoppers from over 200 shows! Includes: Ain't Misbehavin' • All I Ask of You • Bewitched • Camelot • Don't Cry for Me Argentina • Edelweiss • I Dreamed a Dream • If I Were a Rich Man • Memory • Oklahoma • Send in the Clowns • What I Did for Love • more.
00240046..$49.99

The Ultimate Christmas Fake Book – 5th Edition

This updated edition includes 275 traditional and contemporary Christmas songs: Away in a Manger • The Christmas Song • Deck the Hall • Frosty the Snow Man • A Holly Jolly Christmas • I Heard the Bells on Christmas Day • Jingle Bells • Little Saint Nick • Merry Christmas, Darling • Nuttin' for Christmas • Rudolph the Red-Nosed Reindeer • Silent Night • What Child Is This? • more.
00240045 ....$24.95

The Ultimate Country Fake Book – 5th Edition

This book includes over 700 of your favorite country hits: Always on My Mind • Boot Scootin' Boogie • Crazy • Down at the Twist and Shout • Forever and Ever, Amen • Friends in Low Places • The Gambler • Jambalaya • King of the Road • Sixteen Tons • There's a Tear in My Beer • Your Cheatin' Heart • and hundreds more.
00240049 ....$49.99

The Ultimate Fake Book – 4th Edition

Includes over 1,200 hits: Blue Skies • Body and Soul • Endless Love • A Foggy Day • Isn't It Romantic? • Memory • Mona Lisa • Moon River • Operator • Piano Man • Roxanne • Satin Doll • Shout • Small World • Speak Softly, Love • Strawberry Fields Forever • Tears in Heaven • Unforgettable • hundreds more!
00240024 C Edition $49.95
00240026 B♭ Edition..$49.95
00240025 E♭ Edition $49.95

The Ultimate Pop/Rock Fake Book – 4th Edition

Over 600 pop standards and contemporary hits, including: All Shook Up • Another One Bites the Dust • Crying • Don't Know Much • Dust in the Wind • Earth Angel • Every Breath You Take • Hero • Hey Jude • Hold My Hand • Imagine • Layla • The Loco-Motion • Oh, Pretty Woman • On Broadway • Spinning Wheel • Stand by Me • Stayin' Alive • Tears in Heaven • True Colors • The Twist • Vision of Love • A Whole New World • Wild Thing • Wooly Bully • Yesterday • more!
00240099 ....$39.99

Fake Book of the World's Favorite Songs – 4th Edition

Over 700 favorites, including: America the Beautiful • Anchors Aweigh • Battle Hymn of the Republic • Bill Bailey, Won't You Please Come Home • Chopsticks • Für Elise • His Eye Is on the Sparrow • I Wonder Who's Kissing Her Now • Jesu, Joy of Man's Desiring • My Old Kentucky Home • Sidewalks of New York • Take Me Out to the Ball Game • When the Saints Go Marching In • and hundreds more!
00240072 ....$22.95